NEW CANAAN LIBRARY

3 1457 00296 ☑ S0-AEH-573

WITHDRAWN

⑥
3/13/03

NEW CANAAN LIBRARY

OCT 2 6 1999

eye on the sea

Eye on the Sea

REFLECTIONS ON THE BOATING LIFE

Mary Jane Hayes

BREAKAWAY BOOKS
NEW YORK CITY
1999

797.12
H

Eye on the Sea: Reflections on the Boating Life
Copyright 1999 by Mary Jane Hayes
ISBN: 1-891369-06-7
Library of Congress Catalog Card Number: 99-72375

Published by Breakaway Books
P.O. Box 1109
Ansonia Station
New York, NY 10023
(800) 548-4348

Breakaway Books are distributed by:
Consortium Book Sales & Distribution
1045 Westgate Drive
Saint Paul, MN 55114

These essays appeared, in slightly different form, in the following publications: "On the Sea" in *Lookout;* "On Boating" in *Invitation to Boating;* "On Boats" in *Lookout;* "On the Wind" in *Cruising World;* "On My Favorite Harbor" in *The Boston Herald Magazine;* "On Being Afraid" in *Boating;* "On the Best Things in Boating" in *Boating;* "On the Debit Side of Boating" in *Boating;* "On Objectivity" in *Boating;* "On Names" in *New England Offshore;* "On the Monochromatic" in *Boating;* "On the Maine This Mariner Loves" in *Maine Life;* "On the Unexpected" in *Boating;* "On Prologues and Epilogues" in *New England Offshore;* "On Spring Afloat" in *The Patriot Ledger;* "On Summer" in *The Boston Herald Magazine;* "On Exploring" in *The Practical Sailor;* "On Nautical Night Visions" in *Cape Cod Life;* "On Rude Realities" in *The Patriot Ledger;* "On an August Gale" in *Yachting;* "Black Zero Fog" in *Coastal Cruising;* "On the Sublime" in *The Patriot Ledger;* "On the Wind in the Rigging" in *The Boston Globe;* "On Our First Homeport" in *New England Offshore;* "On Dinghyology" in *The Patriot Ledger;* "On the Captain and Crew" in *The Boston Globe;* "On Salty Dogs" in *Coastal Cruising;* "On Autumn Sailing" in *Lookout;* "On a Sojourn South" in *Offshore;* "On Creative Accommodation" in *Sail.*

FIRST EDITION

Contents

For Warren, husband and skipper

"The winds and waves are always
on the side of the ablest navigators."
—Edward Gibbon

Eye on the Sea

I CAME TO THE SEA VIA AN INTIMATE ACQUAINTance with the land and the air. The land from having walked outdoors daily for several miles for most of my life; the air from employment as an airline stewardess in the pre-jet days. Flying all over New England with Northeast Airlines, usually at an altitude of two thousand to ten thousand feet and frequently in windy mountain passes, I learned, in a very immediate way, about the elements and their capriciousness. This experience served me well after my marriage to a man who is a mariner to the marrow of his bones.

Together we cruise the eastern seaboard from Canada to Florida; today aboard *Sea Story II,* our Grand Banks thirty-six-foot trawler yacht—and after years of boating aboard a variety of vessels, both power and sail.

Surroundings (we have discovered) can at times be almost mystical. One night in Hadley's Harbor on Naushon Island in Massachusetts I was awakened by an unearthly quiet. Rising and going on deck, I stood rapt at the rails. Never had I seen a blacker anchorage or one more still or sown with stars. So seamless was the union of heavens and harbor that sky was water and water sky. We were moored as they mingled in the Milky Way.

Conversely, we have been thrashed and pounded unmercifully—far at sea and close to home. Any mariner who has negotiated the Hog Island Channel at the west end of the Cape Cod Canal often enough is aware that it can be a vicious fetch. Now and then heading west, knowing we had a good, sound ship beneath us, and reducing our speed from eleven to eight knots, we have plowed into that gut with a full current running and against a stiff, southwest blast. Always ruder than it looks, the slop has caused our vessel's bow to be buried repeatedly in steep, standing seas of eight feet to ten feet (with troughs the width of a knife blade), and spray to be hurled over our flybridge fifteen feet above.

Fair weather or foul, aesthetics are what speak to me most deeply on the water. The lovely lean of a sailboat heeling is boating as spectacle. So are spinnakers billowing out and moving in unison as they compete in a race. (And how moving it is to be immersed in the majestic motion at the start of a contest, as you weave in and out of the jockeying windships.) Magnificent powerboats can qualify as panoply; along with ferries and freighters and tugs-with-tow and workboats, whose welter of gear is both rugged and pert.

Sunrise at sea is always a wonder. So are sundowns and evenings of a rose-petal perfection. There are luminosities that are fantastic—literally: mists of spun gold rising in sparkling clouds or ghostly mirages manufactured by fog. Not to mention the marvels attending the night—a harvest moon in early summer; anchor lights at the tops of spars; an assortment of aids-to-navigation winking and twinkling; onyx waters; jeweled coasts.

Sometimes prospects supply the enchantment. Many a harbor is a garden spot with a tidy green park adjacent to the sea. Here, headlands rear as romantic as Cornwall's; there, rivers appear as silver as mirrors, or marshes glow a vibrant rouge.

Youngfry and pets afloat add their own perky dimension; along with the more prosy note supplied by grown-ups "messing about" their boats (in all the ordinary, necessary, and satisfying tasks of "keeping" their craft).

Among the scores of other images varying the mariner's milieu are the many bridges spanning some of the waterways we transit, plus islands and beaches and a bevy of basins, each different from the next. Not forgetting the schools of fish that ripple and dimple the waters close aboard or the flocks of birds veering and swooping or stitching the skies over our heads.

The seasons themselves instill succeeding accents of glamour and interest—spring with its spanking horizons; summer's mothlike swarms of craft; the fiery foliage of autumn stamping the shorelines of sapphire ports; winter's dazzling clarity and falls of snow mantling quiet yacht yards with their rows of cradled boats.

All part of a constantly changing and infinitely rewarding panorama for the eye fixed on the sea.

On the Sea

"DAT OLE DEVIL, SEA," O'NEILL CALLED IT IN ONE of his plays. To Felix Riesenberg the sea was a seducer, a "careless, lying fellow," whose proper symbol was a sultan. Swinburne, on the other hand, thought of the sea as feminine, as "the great sweet mother." So did Shakespeare, who wrote of "bauble boats" sailing on her "patient breast." Likened by others to mountains, pastures, prairies—to potter's fields—the sea has also been dismissed as a "melancholy waste." The poet Homer described the sea as "wine dark"; other writers have portrayed it in every shade of gray, of green, of blue. Branded as "indifferent" by many, among them Joseph Conrad, who wrote that he had "known the sea too long to believe in its respect for decency," the sea has likewise been deemed ageless and eternal. "Who can say of a particular sea," mused Thomas Hardy, "that it is old? Distilled by the sun, kneaded by the moon, it is renewed in a year, in a day, or in an hour."

The sea has attracted as well as repulsed. "There is nothing so desperately monotonous," growled James Russell Lowell. An English writer held that the sea was at its best at London, near midnight, when one was seated in an easy chair before a glowing fire. Columbus, by contrast, enjoyed "long stretches of pure delight such as only a seaman may know," according to S. E. Morison, his biographer and himself an impassioned man of the salt. Who can measure the pleasure experienced by the myriads who flock to the water every summer, or explain the force that has drawn them there? So subtle is the relation between the tides of the ocean and the life of man, it is said that along the east coast of England it was believed that most deaths occurred at ebb tide. The sea has inspired Coleridge, Kipling, Melville; it has figured in the canvases of Winslow Homer, in Debussy's "La Mer."

For me, the sea is an element with which I experience a vital relation. There are times when I hate it. The sea can be tedious, uncomfortable, frightening. I have loathed its sometimes abominable motion, and blanched before its ruthlessness. I have come off it with an eye famished for variety. The sea has chilled me to my marrow, and all but roasted my flesh. It has drugged me to stupefaction. The ocean thus endured has also been relished. Some mornings—some passages —are literally divine, and on them one can comprehend the origin of the adjective *heavenly*. The sea has nourished patience in me, courage, self-control. It has introduced me to topographies so exotic I have felt like Sinbad. I have beat on the sea, I have reached, I have run; I have known the glory of a keel's "plowing air." The sea has limbered my body and restored my soul.

Of all my feelings for the sea, the one that runs the deepest is concern. Concern that we not despoil its beauty with our debris or pollute its purity with our wastes. Cousteau and Heyerdahl encountered such damage in midocean; I have seen it for myself in Boston Harbor. Gazing there, one summer (years ago now), at waters fouled to the color of axle grease, I was shamed and sorrowed and made acutely aware that the sea—"the rough, rude sea"—the vast and furious ocean "wherein the whale swims minnow-small" —is, at bottom, like the earth and like the air, at our mercy.

On Boating

I DON'T KNOW HOW MANY TIMES A CRUISE I murmur to myself: "How beautiful!" Not everything is, of course. The pollution in a number of harbors and rivers isn't beautiful, nor are those days at sea when heat and haze hang like a miasma over land and water. I know that somewhere along the way of any extended cruise my family and I are going to have to put up with sun-sore eyes and short tempers, with horseflies, gnats, and sultry basins. But those are the thorns on the rose of cruising, not its blossom.

Sifted of its imperfections boating to me is romance and challenge. It is taking a step backward in a comfort sense to deepen and hone your general experience. It is rough crossings when all aboard are united in a kind of tension of passage; and days when the sea is so smooth the sailboats you pass seem to be sailing on themselves.

It is the wheel of the seasons, each with its gifts. It is bleak, sea-fever days in spring, and spanking ones in June when you glide along in the troughs of the rollers, your ensign whipping rudely behind you. It is zipping down the middle of some sound or other in midsummer, sitting on the bow, breathing deep of sea and sky. It is that perfect day or two in September when color is absolute; each opaline one in late October when cruising has about it a kind of twilight quietude. It is those last few mornings when you go down to find piers and boat rimed with frost, a wintry smoke coming off the river that is your course out to the sea.

Boating is boats, from the humblest pleasure dinghy to the finest poem in fiberglass or wood. It is all the draggers that you pass—of such trim or derelict beauty—and the lobster boats: blue, green, white, piled high with wrack-colored pots. It is the aproned lobstermen upon them, no matter what the weather, matter-of-factly pulling their pots. It is the solid net of buoys they've lain, "mining" every inch of your coast.

Boating is harbors—Quissett, a New England mini Tahiti, and Beverly, where you dock in the shadow of a McDonald's hamburger stand.

It is every seagull on every buoy, piling, dock; and all the old dogs calmly astride the bows of boats.

It is a big breakfast after a cold, rough, rainy run home; and a last cup of coffee on the flying bridge along with a sunset by Maxfield Parrish.

Boating is other boatmen, from the ones who rarely leave the dock to those yellow-slickered Vikings heading with relish out onto that dark, wind-whipped water that you are quitting with relief. It is also the cheerful Canadian who pumps your fuel; the shrewd Yankee who repairs your boat.

Boating is one child flying around on the time-polished ponies at Oak Bluffs, her cheeks as pink as the shorts she is wearing, crying: "I could stay *here* all day!" While the other is seated cross-legged on the bow, patiently catching fish after fish. It is the skipper all of us trust and with whom we venture gladly out onto that vast playground that offers us such a heady and sometimes hazardous game.

On Boats

THE FIRST BOAT I EVER HAD EXPERIENCE OF WAS my (then future) father-in-law's dory, put into the water off North Truro every summer, fresh as a sprig of new mint. The second (properly a ship) was the liner of the old Furness Warren Line that took me to Europe; the third, the *New Amsterdam* that brought me back. The fourth was a chartered cabin cruiser, the cruise itself an experience roughly equivalent to being thrown off a horse on your first mount. With my fifth and sixth boats I came into my own—literally—their being our thirty-one-foot cabin cruiser *Lady Mary* and, later, our twenty-eight-foot sailboat *Serena*. From their decks (and later still those of our two Grand Banks trawler yachts, a thirty-two-footer first and now a thirty-six)—like Henry Higgins with his Eliza—I have not only "grown accustomed to" but fallen in love with boats.

All kinds of boats—from dinghies clustered at their dink docks like hungry ducklings around their mothers to the most majestic and elegant sloops and yawls. Boats, I have discovered, are as various as people, and, like the latter, each should be appreciated for itself. Thus I have loved the sight of snub-nosed tugs and portly ferries, of windjammers, whalers, and old warships, of cat-boats and cabin cruisers, of lobster boats—each with her steadying sail and little squall of gulls.

The snappiest boat I ever saw was a little red, white, and blue dory with stars and stripes paint-ed on her oars, glimpsed once in the South River of Marshfield, Massachusetts. The sorriest (also in the South River) was a half-sunken scow, all splintered wood and peeling paint and the color of a moldy peach. The most impressive in terms of size and condition are the motoryachts of one hundred feet and more encountered in the Intra-coastal Waterway from Virginia to Florida. The most memorable—not one, but a handful of superb sailboats met here and there over the years for which there are no words. By far the most appealing, however, have been the host of "ordinary" boats you see every day in any harbor, filled with children, pets, assorted relatives and friends, lovers, and just about everybody else. (Like Sandburg's Hungarian beer drinkers under the trees, of all boaters they seem to me the happiest.)

As boats have gifted me with a myriad of images, so have they with some matchless minutes. One of the most fascinating (and rudest) days I ever spent aboard one was on a forty-foot trap boat called the *Helen* when the tuna were running off Provincetown. The headiest was a sail down the length of Penobscot Bay, heeling all the way—to starboard a long, undulating line of blue-green mountains and hills, to port a dozen other sailboats, likewise heeling, each etched neatly in a peacock-colored sea. The most serene was a cruise down Maine's Fox and Deer Island Thorofares on our own *Lady Mary* under perfect powerboat conditions: sun, no sea, a light breeze, with now and then a huge fair-weather cloud for an umbrella. And for drama, nothing has exceeded the frightening (and exciting!) slug we made across Nantucket Sound one sloppy October afternoon with unexpected frontal winds of fifty knots, against which we beat for five hours.

Of all the boats I have ever experienced, the most touching, I think, was the *Australia,* housed in a state of disrepair in a shed at Mystic, Connecticut (there being at the time a lack of money and skills to repair her). As one extreme will sometimes suggest another, so her vulnerable condition and attitude focused for me a human and very moving truth: that boats—beneath their infinite variety—are but one (and one of the most versatile and inspiring) of the outward expressions of the spirit of man: and in particular his courage, his curiosity and ingenuity, his desire to be challenged—his capacity for delight.

On the Wind

WIND IS THE MOST IMPORTANT FACTOR IN BOATing. Visibility is controlled by the wind; so are sea conditions and air temperature (and to a degree, sea temperature). The wind can add to current. It affects the way of a boat. On the water, the wind is omnipotent.

Part of the wind's dominion lies in its fickleness. The wind springs up, it dies down; it blows from this direction or from that. There is too much wind or not enough wind, or just the right amount. (We net, we figure, eight hours of perfect sailing out of any two-week cruise.) The wind that may be ignored on the land is disregarded on the water at one's peril. Every boater should know what the wind is now and what the wind is expected to be. (A wise one will invest in a weather radio, and also will add and subtract ten knots to and from any forecast.)

Capricious in action, the wind is a crazy quilt as to character. Here in New England, the prevailing wind is southwest. A fair-weather wind, it is accompanied by hazy visibility. Winds from the east often are malevolent. Even inland, the scent of the east wind brings with it an image of gray seas piling in, of conditions at once ruthless and invigorating. Days with the clarity and sparkle of jewels are the gift of the northwest wind, which is dry and which follows a frontal passage. Winds from the west (and directly out of the south) are warm and beguiling.

The wind can be an imp. Opposing the current, it can whip the mouth of a river into a maelstrom. The wind can turn the weather dour after a spanking beginning. Or halt a race in its course. The wind can roil conditions just enough to make you wonder if you ought to proceed. It can blight your vacation with rain or fog. Satisfying the "stinkpotter" with just enough of itself to make a cooling breeze, it will frustrate the "ragman" who is longing for twelve to fifteen knots.

Those who are drawn to the water are drawn

to the wind and to the challenge in it. In an age of plastic and blacktop, of comfort and routine (with their power to deaden), the wind is a means to being, to feeling deeply. Against the wind we can sound our strengths and discover our limitations. We can enjoy the elements as we rarely can on the buffered land where our relationship to them is usually indirect. Inherent in the wind are both drama and delight. We have seen the sea so dark with an approaching squall it was almost black. We have witnessed vicious fronts with lurid skies, drenching rains, and lightning on bizarre display. We have battled winds of fifty knots. Conversely, we have creamed along at seven knots, feeling, with Homer, as if we were walking on wings and treading in air. We have run home from Maine before a northwest wind in the middle of July. We have laid our sail like a cheek against the sea.

For a week in winter jackets (in midsummer), thank the wind. For light and air so clear you can almost see tomorrow, thank the wind. For your point of sail, thank the wind. For cleaving an ocean undisturbed by so much as a ripple, thank the wind. (Or for having to mush and crash through turbulent waters as best you can.) For a mind gone as numb as your limbs, thank the wind. For apprehension and alarm and disgust at the extreme discomfort being thrust upon you, thank the wind. For pride in enduring, thank the wind. For throbbing pulses and singing nerves and the knowledge that it is *your* strength, *your* judgment, *your* skills that are commanding conditions and heartening the crew, thank the wind. For the wind is omnipotent.

On My Favorite Harbor

My favorite harbor is no particular harbor, but rather aspects of every harbor I've ever entered.

My favorite harbor is the one I'm most familiar with—my home port, that is, formerly the North River of Scituate, Massachusetts, now the harbor of Scituate itself.

Sometimes my favorite harbor is a Yankee classic: Like Barnstable, Edgartown, Camden, or Quissett, it is graced with handsome houses and tasteful gardens on streets that are shaded by oaks and elms.

Or else it may exhibit an almost scrimshaw austerity: its cottages, like those that line the sands of the shore at Green Harbor, modest for the most part and stark as if carved from bone.

On occasion my favorite harbor is a pristine basin girded by spruce—is the virginal and haunting Roque Island.

At others it is a spectacle (and *joie de mer* itself!), such as you experience in Marblehead, with boats in front of you, around you, behind —and Abbott Hall rising like a sort of Mont-St.-Michel above the town.

My favorite harbor can be as panoramic as Boothbay, as majestic as Somes Sound on Mount Desert (which is a vast theater for a random gull), or as honky-tonk as Onset or Oak Bluffs.

Today my favorite harbor might be Vineyard Haven, deft as a canvas by a Dutch master; tomorrow it will be the doughty Gloucester or Menemsha or Mackerel Cove on Bailey's Island.

Now and then my favorite harbor will be a city, will be the port of Boston or Portland, Maine, or the elegant (and enterprising) Newport, Rhode Island.

With its Victorian ambience (lacking only Teddy Roosevelt beaming over the veranda of the grand hotel on Star Island), Gosport on the Isles of Shoals is my favorite harbor. So, too, is Mystic as it re-creates another era even farther in the past.

My favorite harbor is the one that comes as a complete surprise: as did the borough of Stonington, Connecticut, toured on an afternoon in late August, the tang of fallen leaves delighting us as we wandered its comely streets.

My favorite harbor is the one I'm going to sail to *someday:* Monhegan, Matinicus, or Grand Manan. It is also the forbidding grandeur of that landfall in Greenland, or the verdant blue-green peaks of an anchorage in the Grenadines that I will only read about and probably never attempt.

My favorite harbor is one-of-a-kind, is Cohasset with its echoes of Henry James; or Hadley's Harbor, suggestive at twilight—as a red sun sets behind the great stone mansion commanding its heights (and horses graze by the water's edge)— of a Gothic romance.

My favorite harbor is almost any harbor in September, the hulls of the vessels that remain varnished by a mellow sun. Or Nantucket in October with the manager of the Boat Basin inviting us to take our pick of slips. Or Plymouth in May, its deep blue water white with winter logs.

"A harbor, even if it is a little harbor, is a good thing," Sarah Orne Jewett once wrote, "since adventurers come into it as well as go out, and

the life in it grows strong, because it takes something from the world and has something to give
in return."

Including, for these mariners, interest, instruc-
tion, and entertainment—along with anticipation
as we embark—and sanctuary upon our return.

On Being Afraid

WHEN WE FIRST BEGAN BOATING I WAS OFTEN afraid on a boat. It wasn't that I distrusted our skipper. Far from it. An eminently responsible man, he had earned our faith in him through his sure judgment and practical skills proven cruise after cruise. My confidence in him was such that I would gladly have cruised right off the edge of the world with him, if that were his pleasure.

No, what I feared in the main was the unknown. Having that kind of soul, I was more apt to fight new experience than welcome it. I was afraid of the indifference of the sea as well—and of chance. Every now and then something—rough water, a three-foot spot, swells—those vast walls of water that had come into some of our gulfs and sounds from the other side of the world—reminded me, with a consequent stab of panic, that there was nothing between our family and extinction but knowledge and a chip of fiber-glass and wood.

I was afraid for our children, never feeling completely free of their supervision, even when both were in their teens. I was anxious for the one prone to motion sickness, and for both when they were going from stern to bow or bow to stern when it wasn't absolutely smooth. I was afraid of a child overboard and us unconscious of it and pulling away. Sometimes my fear was self-ish and it was *me* struggling in the water.

Blessed (and cursed) with a vivid imagination and with the knowledge that there is a first time for everything, I was also afraid of being seasick, something I'd never yet been. Would I ever be numbered among those miserable wretches, I wondered, wailing that I'd rather be dead? I feared my husband's sudden incapacitation and my possible inability to take over (though this was being remedied by boating courses and prac-tical lessons in boat handling). I was afraid of being enclosed in the cabin when underway, pre-ferring the deck no matter how terrible the sea.

I was afraid of that sporadic loss of equilibrium that comes from absorbing too much sun (or from too much bobbing and rolling), when you feel as if your brains are aboil, and you can think of boating only with disgust.

I was afraid of collision and fire at sea and exploding at the dock when fueling—though there we were especially careful to be careful. I was afraid of the fog that distorted, disoriented, and magnified—that could make a seagull look like a cabin cruiser until you were almost on top of him, and an echo chamber out of your little quarter-mile cone of visibility. I was afraid of the freak squalls that caused disasters, of fierce currents surging through rocky passages. I was afraid of the occasional whale in our waters that could overturn our boat, of hitting submerged logs and other debris, of our propellers becoming entangled in one of the myriad of lobster pots that honeycomb our sea.

Now, after many years of cruising, I still "suffer the possibilities" to a greater degree or less (depending on the circumstances); can still spend an occasional sleepless night rehearsing the arduous adventure of the day to come.

I admit to these fears because I am not mastered

by them. Common sense, thank goodness, has always prevailed. Ours is usually one of the first boats in the water in our harbor, one of the last ones out, and we probably range farther most seasons than anyone else.

Though dread is sometimes one's leitmotif, to *dare* can be one's theme.

On the Best Things in Boating

As in life, so the best things in boating are free and confined to no season. Among my gifts from the sea:

Wind-filled rushes twinkling dryly . . . a bone-white beach . . . one sail slipping into the horizon . . . any of those charming little towns founded on the sea, whose streets slope steeply down to the water . . . wakes wide as bridal trains and waves curving neatly away from a bow . . . a Memorial Day weekend that for once is lovely . . . the Cape Cod Canal (which is never boring no matter how many times you pass through it) . . . the green banks of June . . . a huge orange moon, resting on a little black cloud and sending a swath of peach across water that minnows are dimpling . . . lapping wavelets inducing sleep . . .

. . . a string of storybook days . . . Cape Neddick looking dreamy in the sun . . . pretty Pumpkin Island Light, as apt an accent to Eggemoggin Reach as is the cherry atop a banana split . . . spinnakers like puff pastries . . . dinghies following sailboats like faithful household pets . . . flemished lines . . . a hatch full of stars . . .

. . . petrels rising en masse from the surface of the sea like a flashy checkerboard . . . the light on the Cuckolds winking smartly through the fog . . . piers piled with pots, and sheds "raining" buoys . . . and jellyfish as suddenly thick around you as the noodles in a can of chicken soup . . . the *Scotia Prince* leaving Portland, lit up like a jewel . . .

and then a sun resolved of all but blessing . . . cradles like abandoned cannons in grass yellow as corn (and beyond a molten sky specked with migrating birds) . . . a sea so deep a blue it is almost cruel . . . warm hands and dry feet . . . and mugs of hot coffee or soup . . . sunsets with a wintry cast . . . the eternal clammers . . . visibility so exact you are seeing, it seems, to the end of the world . . . an empty ocean (but just for a while).

On the Debit Side
of Boating

I ONCE OBSERVED TO MY FAMILY THAT THE DEBIT side of cruising the coast of Maine was the rollers, Rockland (because of the odor from a fertilizer factory that was operating at the time), and the many unreadable can buoys. (Sleeping downwind of a lobster boat can also be something of an experience.) The bitter comes with the sweet, it seems, even in boating.

Have you ever bought a boat and then discovered that the hoses and clamps were a shambles and that the water tank had rusted out? Was your first weekend on that boat a comedy of errors (only in retrospect)? Was your frying pan too

large for your stove? Did said appliance blow up
at its first lighting? Were the next three days con-
sumed in trying to scrub off the dried-on foam
left by the extinguisher you used to douse the
resultant fire? And once in your bunks that night
could nobody sleep because the sheets and blan-
kets you bought new for the boat (instead of the
sleeping bags that you ought to have purchased)
kept coming untucked?

Perhaps like us you have endured such things
and more. I find that I could resign quite cheer-
fully all such episodes as well as any encounter
with what might be called the rude and foolish.
Not just the "rules-of-the-road" rude and foolish
—of which the seas are peppered—but the
thoughtless, marina-side as well. Like the
woman and her teenage daughter at Boothbay
who—between them—occupied a single shower
for an hour and fifteen minutes, fully cognizant
that several others of us were waiting. Or those
yachtsmen who conduct raucous, all-night par-
ties at crowded marinas or leave their halyards to
slap maddeningly, or that occasional arrogant
boater who thinks his behemoth (and bullhorn)
entitle him to preferential treatment.

Sailboaters mustn't particularly like bobbing

endlessly in a powerboat's wake, I think, or having the wind spring up from zero to twenty knots just as they are about to enter a harbor and take down their sails. Likewise trying to them must be those days when the wind is too weak or too strong or from the wrong direction, or fluky and erratic. And *no* boater—no matter what his cruising persuasion—enjoys a bad anchorage or feeling "boatbound" or the summer sun when it has gone malicious—raising sores on his lips and making his face feel as if it has been painted on with his eyes screwed in afterward.

One is perfectly justified (in my opinion) in thinking nineteen straight days of zero visibility in fog a bit much, or sighing a little at the harbor that has no children his own children's ages, or no showers or laundromat or ice or fuel or grocery store or fish market or restaurant or beach or pool when he'd very much like them. If you have wished to wish away following seas large as crocodile's jaws, or that you could be set in gimbals to better come to terms with deep rolling—so have I. Like me, you too would probably banish, if you could, all leaks and litter and those lapses in concentration that result in going aground or hitting bottom or (much worse!) a rock. Were you in charge of cruising circumstances and conditions no doubt no stretch of coast would ever exist without a convenient harbor to duck into; nor would anyone ever have to be towed in or cracked in the head by a door or a boom. And the sun would *always* be shining when guests were aboard.

But boating (alas!) is imperfect, and thus shot through with the inconvenient, the uncomfortable, and the downright dangerous. And yet we who "go down to the sea" in our boats wouldn't give it up. For when all of its debits have been counted, what is left—one finds—is love.

On Objectivity

I HAVE ALWAYS HELD THAT MY FIRST CRUISE— a charter—was my worst cruise. We had been riding a sloppy following sea most of a July afternoon, steering up Buzzard's Bay from Cuttyhunk (an island in the Elizabeth Islands chain just off the coast) to the western entrance of the Cape Cod Canal. Within minutes of turning into the Hog Island Channel, we had been engulfed in a turmoil of angry water caused by the clash of a maximum ebb current from the canal and the onrushing wind and seas sweeping up from the southwest.

That maelstrom had been almost too much for our twenty-six-foot cabin cruiser. My husband had had to swing the boat into the trough, hoping that it would then come back into the angry seas that loomed above us. I remember looking up at solid green walls of water, feeling an intense physical fear and an equally intense pity for the two children (safe ashore with their grandparents, thank goodness!) who, I thought, would soon be without us. Also thinking that we had "had it"—at least so far as the boat was concerned—my husband told me to try and get down into the cabin and get on a life jacket and, for whatever good it might do, start the bilge pump. I don't know how long it took me to accomplish these two simple requests. It seemed forever. The next few minutes, as the twin Chryslers roared and the boat alternately rolled deeply in the trough and crashed forward at an angle to the breaking crests, my husband can remember neither fear nor details. *I* can remember standing beside him hanging on for dear life! Gradually we had worked our way into the lee of Bird Island and shortly thereafter anchored in the unbelievable peace of Marion Harbor. Every dish on board was broken, the cabin was a shambles, we were soaked to the skin.

That that experience didn't queer forever any wish of mine to step foot on a boat I owe to three years' experience as an airline stewardess. Hedgehopping in the New England mountains in the days when flying was still something of an adventure had instilled in me—at least where the elements are concerned—a healthy sense of balance. For I had learned then that the skies, which could toss you viciously about one day, could be millpond smooth the next. Boating, I was sure, like flying, would prove to be a mix.

It has. For every disastrous run there has been an ideal passage, for every port that disappointed, one that surprised and delighted. Two of the finest days we ever enjoyed at sea were followed by two of the thickest fogs. Boating, for us, has been almost an embodiment of Emerson's law of compensation.

The advantages of a balanced attitude are not solely personal. If judgment is the skipper's greatest attribute, then calm is the mate's. From her must flow the reassuring look and word, and that continuous enthusiasm for boating, with all its ups and downs. Though we are careful boaters—paying scrupulous attention to weather forecasts, small-craft advisories, and the like—sometimes the rude is thrust upon us. Forecasts *can* be incorrect; there is always the unexpected, or the worse-than-predicted, or those infrequent occasions when, under pressure of time, perhaps, or an urgent family consideration, some small risks *must* be taken and a port left. As the woman sets the tone in the home, so does she on a cruise, and of disagreeable passages this is particularly true.

I don't know how many times now we have gone by Cleveland Ledge Light, the scene of my first traumatic experience. But every time we do pass that spot, I think of what I would have missed had I quit boating at that juncture, out of discouragement. And I am reminded that what Matthew Arnold once counseled of life—to see it "steadily" and to see it "whole"—is especially true of cruising.

On Names

JAMIBUSPIBIGAGICYNJORIC is the longest (and oddest) name I've yet noticed on a boat. *Flirt* is the perkiest. Both are solutions to a challenge that faces every yachtsman: what to name his boat. Long before we owned a yacht, my husband was keeping a list of possible names for one. Included were: *Sea Haze,* a play on our name and love for the sea; *Camelot,* his favorite song; and *Yankee Peddler,* which he has been (in insurance) most of his working life. None seeming quite right to him at the time of purchase, he decided to name the boat after me. The *Mary,* however, was too plain; the *Mary Jane* sounded too much like a lobster boat; the *Mistress* of the *Mistress Mary* might be confused with "distress" over the radiophone. His final choice was *Lady Mary,* for not only did it sound right, it would look pretty on the transom.

And there are a lot of other *Lady*s out on the sea—among them Jane, Alice, and Marion. There is also many a II, III, or IV of something—which is not a sign of ostentation but deep affection. Though some names are romantic (and a few offbeat), most are homely in the best sense of the word, with a familial connotation. (Now and then one comes upon a tasteless name, which demeans the boat it is supposed to adorn.)

Windships are almost a special case. "The name of a sailboat ought to flow," a young foredeckman once told me. When pressed for his choices, *Williwaw* and *Guinevere* were the ones he posited, which certainly fit his rule. But there is many an appealing exception. One of the most engaging boats in our experience was a pale green C&C twenty-seven-footer named *Puck.* Smaller than most of her sisters in a recent yacht-club flotilla, she was one of the most dauntless and enterprising when it came to appearing at the scheduled rendezvous. (No matter what the weather or sea conditions.) A glance at any yacht-club roster—New York's for

example, where names like *Zest, Madcap,* and *Boo*
stud an otherwise elegant roll—convinces one
that if there is a place in nomenclature for the
"proper," there is room for the saucy as well.

Names, of course, aren't confined to boats.
Where appellations are concerned, coastal New
England is a cornucopia. There are the French
names (like Calais, Orleans and Isle au Haut);
the Indian—of which Annisquam and Sippican
are but two of a mellifluous host; the down-to-
earth Yankee: Prouts Neck, Potts Harbor, Per-
kins Cove. John Bull has left tokens of himself
all over the terrain: in Bristol and Bath, in Newcastle, Greenwich, and Falmouth, in Bullock and
Bunker Coves. Wildlife is generously represent-
ed in names like Deer Isle, Duck Harbor and Eel
Pond; topography defined in others such as
Sandy Bay or High Head.

While some names are perfect for the places they
describe—Corea and Wychmere, for instance, or
Marblehead (not to mention Quick's Hole, which
you are through before you can say)—others are
misleading. The Mudhole, for one, which isn't
anything of the sort, but an attractive cove on the
east side of Great Wass Island, and Junk of Pork
for another, it being a bit of Cornwall in Casco

Bay. (Some of the genealogies of the more colorful names are downright funny. Racketash, which
is Indian, became Ragged Arse before it finally
came to rest as Ragged Island.)

Namewise, a good case could be made for opposites. There are the Goose Islands and their
Goslings; the "His" and "Hers" Ledges (Old Man
and Old Woman) off Maine. Tongue twisters like
Quamquissett and Canapitsit (to say nothing of
the Magaguadavic River) are balanced by the likes
of Sail Rock and Wooden Ball, names simple in the
extreme. If Smuttynose (Island) and the Cow Yard
strike one as a trifle prosy, what could be prettier
than Prettymarsh or Jewell Island or Christmas
Cove on the Damariscotta? (Which is not only
pretty, but proof—as tiny sailboats, thick as mosquitoes, beat about its harbor, crewed by what
looks to one like little more than infants—that in
Maine they "sail them early.") And so graceful is
Flying Mountain (over Somes Sound) that it
almost does!

"Everything means something," the ancients
told us. So what's in a name? People, mostly. Even
in *JAMIBUSPIBIGAGICYNJORIC*—which is a
compilation of some of the letters from each of the
names of her owner's ten children.

On the Monochromatic

THERE IS A BLUE HAZE THAT IS IDYLLIC AND A gray murk that is as depressing as smog. I would speak here of the latter, and also of fog, rainy days aboard, and those times—whatever the season or month—when it is "bleak midwinter" on the sea.

My least-favorite days on the water are those heat-and-haze-enshrouded ones in summer when it seems as if a great cloth has been dropped over the beauty of the world. Not only are they cheerless; there is something ominous about them: One can sense building seas and developing storms behind their milky calm. "Thicks-o-fogs" have kept us confined to piers (and champing at our slip) for days at a time. We have seen whole weeks of our once-a-year cruising vaca-

tion go down in rain; and at least half of our boating experience (or so it seems) has been charac-
terized by what we call "gray paste." In the
Northeast, the boating season is born in the
bleak, expires in the bleak, and is checkered by
the bleak throughout its duration. These conditions correspond roughly to the drudgery in life,
to routine: being nature—as Emily Dickinson
once put it—"without her diadem."

But sweet can be the uses of the unlovely. Such
weather is not without its compensations. Here,
experience not only "worketh patience," but fore-
sight, resourcefulness—a challenge all to the good
these days—and moments of real satisfaction and
delight. I have almost acquired a taste for it.

There is a certain beauty of bleakness, and one
can sometimes sympathize with the poet who
wrote that she loved the look "austere, immaculate, of landscapes drawn in pearly monotones."
(Not to mention the sight of your children's
vibrant, wind-whipped faces almost fierce with
health!) There is also the peace of accepting the
truth that every single minute on a cruise is not
going to be stimulating. On every cruise of any
length there are passages that last forever. (I
remember one such on a cruise to Maine when

it seemed as if we were permanently affixed to a spot just opposite Seguin—that stern, uninviting island just off the Kennebec—which seemed at the time the perfect symbol of the seas we were being tossed about in.)

Bad weather has taught us to be prepared for bad weather. When our children were small, we never left port without an ample supply of paper, pencils, Magic Markers, and a surprise book or magazine or two to be produced when the ingenuity and enterprise of the crew had, for the moment, flagged.

A family knits back into itself with enforced enclosure. Gray, rainy weekends on a boat when you go nowhere—when you read, eat, play Parcheesi or cards, listen to the ballgame or to the swish of rain pimpling the slip and drumming on decks and cabin top—can be snug and cozy. One bonus of such interludes for this boating family used to be that we could include our dog Salty (who wasn't, and who had to spend most of his boating weekends and vacations cruising a local kennel).

Then, too, the dull sharpens your appreciation of the brilliant. There is no joy quite like that of seeing a dismal day grow clear and blue, of watching a bay become a mirror for its islands and clouds, and a solitary tern doing a pas de deux with his own reflection. Food tastes better, somehow, when outside it's raw or stormy. And when you know where you are—and that it isn't going to last long—fog can be fun, its effects as fantastic as those in your childhood edition of *The Arabian Nights*.

One of the most fascinating parts of the cruise we once made to Mystic, Connecticut, was the figureheads. As I stood pondering their magnificent forms in the Stillman Building, I found myself wondering what had tried those sailors of the last century the most on their cruises of two to three years. Had it been the whale? The storm at sea? Or had it been, as it is for most of us today, I believe, the eternal *sameness* of things? Perhaps we are mature as boaters, and persons when we have learned to "rise with grace to the occasion of the ordinary."

On the Maine This Mariner Loves

MAINE IS AS MUCH A STATE OF BEING AS IT IS A place. It appeals most strongly, I believe, to those who relish the realized and the concrete. The essence of its charm is order, and to the nature that seeks it, that quality is nowhere more vividly embodied than in the waters Down East.

The Maine this mariner loves is, first, the Maine of its firs. Here, each spruce is the perfect spruce, and yet packed in such lavish stands you can't see between them. And they exude, those groves, an air of worship, as if each of their spires is raised in praise of its Maker. Indeed, taken as a whole, the coast of Maine is one long hosanna.

The rocks from which these balsams rise are

another of Maine's marvels. Water gouged and sculpted, they are as majestic to me as the Coliseum or Chârtres Cathedral. Not that all of them are grand. Some are tidy slabs inlaid with firs. Others are almost bare, except for the green and purple of their flowers and the white of seagull droppings. Most are fringed with rockweed, circlets of which break off and float to sea like crowns of thorns.

The medium this flotsam litters is romantic. Of course there's fog in Maine, and murk and mush and glop and gloom—and days forbidding as those on the plains in winter. But when the cruising in Maine is good, it's grand. Rollers slope in from the ocean, a deep blue-green in color. Gaff rigs suggest the Orient, as do a rugged shore and a host of schooners slipping in and out of islands and up and down a trove of bays.

The Maine this mariner loves is lonely. East of Schoodic Point stretches country so spartan you would not be in the least surprised to see Eskimos come gliding by in kayaks. And the gods took special care when they fashioned Roque Island in Englishman Bay. (Past Moose Peak Light you voyage. Past rocky little islands crammed with firs. Past Shag and Pulpit Rocks into a basin right out of legend.) Roque is the sort of anchorage where you take bearings on a forked tree and the edge of a line of spruce. And where the peace is so deep you almost feel uneasy.

Boothbay, by contrast, bustles, and yet is no less enchanting. Activity is incessant in this yachting capital and everywhere picturesque. (In Maine, if anywhere, the paradise depicted on the postcards is literal.) What a jolly scene, that harbor on a sparkling summer day! Excursion vessels, jammed to capacity, journey in and out. So do sailboats and powerboats by the dozens, to say nothing of sailing schools that swirl about its waters like coveys of moths. While hotels look fresh under sherbet-colored awnings, islands look dapper under puffy little clouds. And against a screen of firs, each vessel, dwelling, pier, and gull stands out neatly.

If these charms are not enough, you can climb Boothbay's hills in the evening and gaze ten miles out to sea. You can stop and chat for a minute with a lady cutting columbines on one of its back streets. You can shower at its yacht club, all fresh white paint and hanging pots, crowded with geraniums. Or cruise to Christmas Cove around the point, or to East Boothbay or to the New Harbor that is a Down East classic in appearance and spirit.

Maine is a mine of eclectic delights. I even love the Maine you must be careful of: the Maine of ledge and lobster pots and fog—that wily Merlin that bewilders vision while it swallows sound.

Not to mention the Maine I've yet to visit. No single cruise can ever encompass all that coast-line has to offer.

So here's to Maine. Where a sudden lust for a lobster can always be satisfied. Here's to careful gardens and gracious parks and elms like rich fans in Castine. Here's to a lovely cove around each curve. And to dowagers in yachting caps and fish-ermen shoveling bait in a melting pot that works. (Truly *human* human beings, these.) Here's to the Portland that is the Stockholm of New England; and to Mount Desert, our Yankee Hawaii.

Not for me the Grenadines. The compass in the soul of *this* mariner points east.

On the Unexpected

"No one is ever always fortunate," wrote Euripides. Including boaters. Cruising is punctuated with the unexpected, negative as well as positive.

Careful as one may be, no boater is immune to accidents: the bent propeller, the broken mast, the cup of coffee that goes flying. Being whipped across the eyes by the mainsheet is a surprise. So is melting ice overflowing its container and turning your rug into a saturated sponge, or car lights (all night) shining in your windows from a dock. Sometimes it is a stinging rebuke one finds startling, such as the one I once earned from the captain of a Cape Cod trap boat who roared at me to "Git your XX#$%XX hands off the gunwales!" as I clambered aboard—a lesson I never forgot.

A light going inoperative, suddenly, in thick fog . . . a diaphone inaudible until you are just abeam of it . . . the fog heaving up a dory with neither horn nor warning, are likewise alarming. On a trek ashore, could we have predicted our getting temporarily lost on Camden's Mount Battie when the trail we were following petered out? Or that we would go to the wrong side of a spindle in Maine's New Harbor (so bewitched were we by its beauty) and nearly come to grief on a rock?

If boating has its backfires, its incidents and annoyances that leave a sour taste in the feelings, by far the bulk of its surprises are on the light side: a dewy morning after a stormy night . . . deep shade at noon (such as that provided by the Tabernacle at Oak Bluffs, whose rafters also serve as a sanctuary for a myriad of birds) . . . a ride out to your boat under the stars (the face of a clock on shore yellow as a harvest moon), are a delight to the spirit. So is the bill for your diesel fuel, pots set to either side of a channel, and a spotless restaurant in Camden (or anywhere else).

Sometimes the pleasure is personal—your husband turning to you in the middle of Massachusetts Bay (as you spell him at the wheel) and remarking that you steer a straighter compass course than he does, or your son relieving tensions with a cartoon entitled: "The Low Points of Our Cruise." At others it is an insight that arrests. I will never forget the day I first became aware of the physics of sailing and capsizing. (A spanking one in August, I was tacking and jibing over sandflats in a simple little Sunspot, a bare foot of water between her deck and bottom.) Names, too, can give us pause. Among my favorites are Thrumcap, Thread o' Life, and Whaleboat Island, which, with its heavily timbered "bow" and "stern," looks its appellation.

While some examples of the unexpected are homely—the mizzen, for instance, serving as parasol on a hot July day, or the decorated trash cans and bass lockers on Cuttyhunk —others are splendid. Cutting power and shifting into a sail so easy you feel you ought to whisper, or surfing into Castine—its great tree-dotted hills flounced with shadows—are as moving in their way as an epic poem or a great symphony. So is a shaft of sun dropping out of the overcast like a spotlight, and countless other natural effects. To say nothing of those ports that are wellsprings: Northeast

Harbor and New Harbor in Maine (and Somes Sound and the whole Mount Desert area for that matter), Manchester, Quissett, Nantucket, and Barnstable in Massachusetts, and the Edgartown that is a grande dame of a harbor (and Menemsha, her merry little sister) are "happenings" every time we cruise them. As is the passing of Owl's Head Light, the prettiest light in Maine.

If the unexpected sometimes betrays us, it just as often re-creates, and by freshening our responses, helps ensure us against going stale, both as boaters and as persons.

On Prologues and Epilogues

THERE IS A PROLOGUE AND AN EPILOGUE TO every boating season. In the main, the first runs from when you get your boat in the water to about the Fourth of July, the second from Labor Day to when it is hauled. A feeling of hope characterizes the one, fulfillment the other.

A boatyard is a web of life in the spring. It speaks of arrivals and departures, of plans and dreams, of an experience different in texture and kind from the daily round of things. A feeling of being "outward bound" invests the scene, gaiety mingling with the sound of sanding and the scents of paint and creosote. The summer rolls ahead of one like a red carpet. Whenever I'm not busy on our own, I enjoy walking up and down the rows of cradled boats, watching their owners at work on them or reading their names. Some I know I'll never see again, others not until fall.

Then there is the pleasure of your own boat, lying at her slip, clean as a bleached shell. Not only would she have been painted and varnished, her teak decks would have been cleaned and sealed, her seam leaks fixed, every inch of her chromium and glass polished and washed. Fresh, new curtains might have been hung, or she might be sporting a new burgee, canvas flying bridge cover (if a cabin cruiser), or larger stainless-steel water tank. As you survey her you will be vowing that you're not going to make the same mistakes you've made other seasons—which you won't, of course; you'll just make others.

The first few boats in the water (among which yours will be one) are like the first few delegates at a political convention: Though one senses great events and important choices ahead, just now all is still tentative. The empty mooring buoys rise out of the water like flowers reaching for the sun. The air is still nippy and fresh, warm in the lees of your boat, but very brisk indeed when you step from shelter. When not gray and raw as December, these will be days of crisp whites and deep blues. Yours will be the luxury of rediscovering familiar harbors at your leisure—and practically by yourselves. With May and June will come two- and three-day cruises, to harbors filled with lilacs, robins, and elm-shaded inns. When not actually "traveling," there will be races to observe, fish to catch (though you won't hook a single haddock, you will haul in more cod than you can ever use or want), and the desire—if not quite the courage—to swim.

If spring is thus the aperitif of boating, then autumn is its dessert and coffee. Not for anything would we give up those last few months of cruising. More rugged as to weather (after September, that is, which is sublime), they have a more concentrated beauty. How splendid are those mornings when the sea has a heavy, molten gleam on it, and the spray that comes over the bow is cold as ice and bright as diamonds! And those last few days in October as rude in their truth as early April's.

On one such we stood off to render assistance—if it was necessary—to a sailboat coming into our river (the mouth of which is often vicious) on its way to be hauled at our marina. Our help wasn't needed. In they came, two people no longer young—a man and a woman— with weather-beaten faces and woolen caps. That they were enjoying the challenge was obvious by the smiles on their mouths and in their canny, crinkled eyes. A little salute (by way of thanks to us for standing by) and on they went up the river, under power now, absorbed in its navigation. We returned their salute, feeling that autumn—whether of the weather or of experience and years—was indeed "the last for which the first was made."

On Spring Afloat

YOU ARE, YOU FIND, THE FOURTH BOAT ON A
mooring out of a fleet that will swell to a thousand. Though the harbor of Scituate, Massachusetts, in early May is deserted compared to
what it will be a month or two hence, it is not
without life. Draped with seines, draggers loom
in its mouth and then come steadily in. Lobster
boats depart, their decks heaped high with pots. In
hired dories, anglers stud the anchorage or head
offshore aboard the party boat *St. Joseph*. On the
horizon barges and freighters may be spotted,
bound for Boston or the Cape Cod Canal. Like a
large mosquito, a helicopter passes over.

So does an airplane streaming a banner.
Despite the budding trees that border the basin

and a handful of masts being stepped at docks—with its inky waters strewn with winter logs and with temperatures less like spring's than the chill end of September—the port still sports an autumnal aura.

As usual, a few bloopers remind you that you have to reacquaint yourself with procedure. You forget to turn on your gasoline so your engine stalls. Or you hank on your jib upside down (lowering it as soon as raised before anyone detects the gaffe). A crop of gremlins also has to be resolved. Mysteriously, your anemometer registers only in winds of over fifteen knots. Your compass, you notice, has a pronounced forward tilt at certain headings; and your engine is overheating. (The mechanic you fetch discovers that mussels had grown in the inlet of the water pump and way up in the inlet of the thermostat, constricting the flow of cooling water.)

You fine-tune your yacht: adjusting the rigging, tightening stanchions, treating the teak. You wax the fiberglass above decks, glowing when a stranger inquires of your seven-year-old sailboat: "Is it new?" What are new are some additions to her gear, including a "rescue" swim ladder (should someone go overboard) and a new radar.

Now commences the annual waltz with the weather. Like every other mariner, you are well versed in its vagaries. Unhappily, you can count on a gray, cold, rainy spring with four to six week-ends in a row of foul weather just after your vessel is launched and on her mooring. "We've done everything this year but sail," the skipper will mutter disgustedly during this enforced hiatus. "Here it is almost Memorial Day and we haven't even had the jib up!" If, in autumn, you hold your breath against a hurricane assaulting the coast, in spring the danger is a sneak, disastrous gale. When not actually stormy, conditions are apt to be dour and hostile. Stiff winds will lock you into port. Or beat up furiously once you've ventured out. "So much preparation," the first mate will sigh, as she is pitched and tossed on a rough slug whipped by twenty-five-knot winds (and thinking of the house, the yard, the family obligations that had had to be attended to prior to this voyage), "simply to endure." There will be lumpy days when rollers come in from the Atlantic. Others of airs so light you will spend them ghosting in and out of "holes." Not to mention fluky days that seem a year long as up, down, up, down, you hoist or douse sails in response to the breeze or lack of it.

Notwithstanding baleful elements, a good deal of "nuts-and-bolts" boating is accomplished. You fit your life harnesses to yourselves and practice hooking their lines to the cockpit, to the base of the mast, around the bow pulpit. You fly your large genny when more canvas is called for and your cruising chute in zephyrs. For practice you reef and double-reef your main, "heaving to" in a "blow" of seven knots. You sail up to your mooring instead of motoring; and fog is utilized for back-to-basics compass runs.

When the weather is fair, it can be fabulous— literally. As you do in the fall, you delight in the same luminous shores and lower sun; the same sharp horizons and sapphire seas. Merely daysailing outside your own harbor you might be essaying the broad waters of the world. Some days that world seems painted. Blue skies are festooned with fluffy clouds that barely move. On others motion is everywhere you look. In sailboats clawing their way upwind. In your own canvases billowing out as breezes whistle down the slot. In boundless whitecaps gleaming beneath a brilliant sun. If rare, what felicitous sails you sometimes draw! Sails so smooth and easy you feel as light as a feather landing on silk.

Sails that are at once rude and exalted. Harnessed up, surfing south to Plymouth before a north-west wind of thirty knots (and making eight yourself!), you are wholly possessed by the élan of the sport. To say nothing of your local sight-seeing jaunts north to Cohasset or to New Inlet (to the south).

In June the racing resumes. Besides the PHRF and Thunderbird series, there is the Blue Water Regatta, for which boats from a host of Massachusetts ports arrive to take part. How moving are those contests among queens! Full of concentrated poetry at the start as the large and lovely vessels maneuver; wondrous visually when under spinnakers; suggestive of nothing so much as crossed swords as they take off on different tacks. Radio use also increases with the burgeoning traffic. Requests for radio checks are frequent. So are transmissions between the Coast Guard and a passel of mariners (the former addressing the latter with the ubiquitous "Cap"). There are the familiar, crusty voices of Marshfield and Salem Controls (of the New England Surf Patrol); and the childish ones of youngsters, who abuse the channels by getting on and "cutting up." ("Come on, kiddies; get off the radio," reprimands a disgruntled yachtsman. "Go read your manual.")

By the 21st when spring gives way officially to summer, you know that season has indeed "acome"! The harbor that is as ample and cozy as a catboat's cockpit is positively glutted with yachts. In addition to the workboats, to the whalers of the harbormaster and the Mass. Marine Patrol—to the racing machines and the mix of vessels belonging to the fishing aficionados and the other "early-bird" sailors like yourselves, you encounter every conceivable kind of craft. Anchored, on moorings, tied up at slips, crisscrossing the basin, coming in, going out (keeping the channel in a constant state of roil) are Typhoons, Lasers, and Herreshoffs; handsome Egg Harbors and Hatterases; spiffy sportfishermen and trawler yachts; windsurfers, speedboats, catamarans; commodious launches crammed with figures; dinghies and runabouts thick as water lilies on a pond. And all amid a meld of smacking halyards and humming motors, of slapping wavelets and squawking gulls.

Which pitch won't diminish till Labor Day falls.

On Summer

SUMMERTIME—AND THE CRUISIN' IS EASY, AND its reason, really, for being.

Summer is your two-week cruise to Maine, maybe, or to Cape Cod and the Islands, or to Newport and Mystic. It is fueling and buying ice and searching out a laundromat—and cruising right up to a restaurant to dine. Summer is homely little variety stores and choice S. S. Pierce–type markets and elegant gift shops dealing only in the select. (Also rakish ones dispensing plastic trinkets.) Summer is too many postcards to choose from.

Summer is five windjammers strung out in a row leaving Camden. And behemoths, one upon another, at Newport and Nantucket. It is a gaff-rigged yawl flashing like diamonds in the sun.

Summer is a horizon daubed with spinnakers, and "hundred-harbored Maine" absorbing boats as easily, it seems, as a garden does plants. And summer is ferry and excursion boats by the dozens, and barges and freighters with no one (or so you'd swear) aboard them. And the splendid arrival of the New York Yacht Club at Oak Bluffs, cries of: "Where's Charlie? Where's George? Has anyone heard from the *Wee Winks* yet?" filling the air.

Summer is days soft as a Cézanne and "smoky southwesters" that *finally* blow themselves out. It is a day so perfect you use seven of its diamond hours to run all the way home. Summer is early departures and breathless noons and harbors at twilight—each boat unspooling a bolt of blue silk as it cruises slowly by. And summer is seagulls screeching and wheeling low over the water and then coming to rest in dories or as ruching on roofs. Summer is lobster buoys strewn like confetti across harbor mouths.

Summer is the unexpected repair work that reminds you (not that you need it!) that a boat is "a hole in the water into which you pour money." It is strange movie houses and faces copper as pennies and friendships struck up and as quickly surrendered. Summer is anticipation, absorption, exhaustion: plans scrapped by the weather (among other causes) or happily carried out. Summer is being underway for so long your bones are turning rpms, or tying up (as you swiftly discover) too early. Summer is busily sightseeing or blissfully doing nothing. It is taking your father out fishing or your aunt for a ride.

Summer is pan-fried sole and a gin-and-tonic (or a Coke) and the delicious scent of steak sizzling on someone else's hibachi. Summer is Bass Harbor Light set amid its battalions of spruce. Summer is seas smooth as pearl-colored oil or blue as a colleen's eyes. It is each little pine-packed island, sprigged with flowers and frosted with clouds.

Summer is gorgeous horseflies with vicious bites and midges—making up in numbers (and a sense of purpose) for what they lack in size. It is coots, cormorants, porpoises—and the whiskered, mischievous seals sunning themselves on ledges or playing hide-and-seek with your boat. Summer is the bleak splendor of the Isles of Shoals. And the blue and cream of chicory and Queen Anne's lace popping out like corn in Block Island's fields. It is insects buzzing deep in the grasses at Menemsha; the latter's fishing fleet and public beach and mountains of scallop shells.

And summer is the wave of a stranger in the Cape Cod Canal (or Eggemoggin Reach or Fishers Island Sound). It is donning a lifejacket and swimming through crystal-clear water to a perfect cove. And then looking up—so romantic is the spot—half expecting to see Long John Silver come hobbling over a dune.

Summer is endless, and over all too soon.

On Exploring

FOR SOME PEOPLE ALL THE JOY LIES IN THE mechanics of getting there. But for me a cruise is only half itself without the exploring. By exploring I don't mean an empty ticking off of a port's points of interest (though many of the latter certainly are fascinating), but a grasping of its essence.

In over twenty years of cruising the East Coast of the United States and particularly New England, explore we have: by bus around Martha's Vineyard, by ferry to Nantucket, by taxi on Block Island, by rented car at Mount Desert. But my favorite means of exploration is still by foot, experience having taught me that a walk is more revelatory of a place than anything else. I always feel a little

sorry for those who hug harbors and their environs. The truth of Camden, Maine, for instance,
is not just in its harbor but up on its hills. As I
stood on one of them one evening—looking
down through a garden and some trees to the little spruce-clad islands dotting the bay beneath—
the chirrup of birds mingled with the chimes of a
church. In that instant I *plumbed* Camden.
Similarly, in Oak Bluffs on Martha's Vineyard,
one can step from the razzamatazz of the harbor
(and of the present) into a quaint little pocket of
history by merely strolling down any one of a
number of lanes and onto its Tabernacle
grounds. Or on Nantucket follow bricks and
cobbles into romance. One of our family's most
vivid boating memories is of our first climb up
Cuttyhunk's "lookout hill" one summer
evening. As we wended our way up its steep,
Bermuda-like road, other allusions—triggered
by the ever-changing prospect—succeeded one
another like the reels of a film. They were as
nothing to what awaited us at the top. To have
missed that vista would have been to have
missed an overview of an entire cruising ground.

Basically, I am a traveler who gets where she's
going by boating. My husband is a mariner who

cares passionately about the passage but only incidentally about the destination. Leaving him to "mess happily" about our boat (since our children are now grown and we parents cruising mainly by ourselves), I plunge as happily into the scenery. Though I loved sightseeing with our offspring, I also enjoy these solitary treks. I like the anonymity conferred on me by a "strange" locale—the little recess from relationships such places afford. I like being able to wander where I want to—and to talk or not talk—answerable to nobody and nothing but my own fancy. I like being a "sponge" and soaking up local color with nobody the wiser. Such interludes are a restorative to one whose immediate life (like most peoples') is all too often crowded and demanding.

Prior to any voyage, I write the chambers of commerce of all the ports we intend to visit, requesting maps of their city and any brochures detailing points of interest. (In preparation for our two-week cruise to Rhode Island one summer, I wrote, for example, to Wickford, Bristol, Newport, and Block Island.) Ever alert to possible future voyages and destinations, I also avail myself of any magazine article, newspaper clipping, or leaflet that might prove helpful (such as

"The Essex Adventure," a brochure picked up in a restaurant in Gloucester detailing tourist attractions on Boston's North Shore), which material then joins all the other data saved in what is now a bulging packet of such "aids-to-exploring." The "boning up" that is done as a matter of course before every one of our sojourns includes, as well, the use of cruising manuals and books. Our first spring as yachtsmen my husband purchased a copy of Julius Wilensky's *Cape Cod—A Thorough Boating Guide to Vineyard Sound, Nantucket Sound, Cape Cod Bay, Buzzards Bay*. At first I said I wasn't going to read it, as I wanted to form my own impressions of places, but I soon changed my mind—discovering that for every delight you might stumble across there would be ten you would miss. Before the end of the summer that volume had become a Bible to us. So have many other books since.

Yes, I'm all for the exploring of ports. But there is also something to be said for the advantages of exploring simply by boat itself. Ninety percent of the grace and grandeur of the Maine (or any) coast is missed, I'm convinced, by the landlubber. Try hiring a car on Mount Desert Island, and then follow up that tour with one on a boat! To see a port by water is to see it fresh—and this applies as much to the familiar as the foreign. The Boston that you think you know like the back of your hand is an entirely new thing when seen from the sea. So is the Scituate or Cohasset or Plymouth or Green Harbor. And ports being no more static than life itself, the boatman who is confined by the size of his boat or pocketbook to the same stretch of coast hasn't necessarily lost out. If he's wise and Thoreau-like, he can make up in depth of experience for what he lacks in scope.

Exploring by boat includes for us the use of excursion vessels and ferries. Long ago we lost any disdain we might have felt for such junkets, learning that they are a wonderful way of getting a bird's-eye view of a port or portion of coast. Also, now and then the captain and first mate need a break from being responsible and concentrated and find it fun to resign themselves to the knowledgeable hands of somebody else. Dinghy tours of a harbor, and particularly those enjoyed in summer twilights, in which you view other vessels up close and poke into all the nooks and crannies you'd otherwise miss from your mooring, also help to re-create one's cruising self.

Another most pleasant aspect of exploring is the

yet-to-be-explored. As ports are inexhaustible, so are coasts. There is always the Hell's Gate or Quahog Bay you didn't get to see, or the cove or island denied you because of time or conditions. Not to mention the whole wonderful world of dreaming! If I could go anywhere I chose it would be to Nova Scotia and Newfoundland and even beyond. Or by slow boat of some sort down the canals and rivers of Europe.

Camus once wrote that no great work of art was ever based on contempt. Neither should tourism be. If you have to approach a place with a bias, I used to counsel our children, let it be that of appreciation. All places instruct—if only negatively. Most, however, enrich.

On Nautical Night Visions

SOMETIMES NIGHT IS THE MOST BEAUTIFUL PART of a sailor's day.

I think of village greens steeped in the gold of summer evenings. Of dinghies and daysailers inverted, and lining a shore. Of hulls in a harbor gleaming as if the port had been oiled.

I think of twilights with a lilac cast; of others so rosy even their gulls are tinted pink. Of coral-colored clouds and grasses billowing silkily in the breeze. Of radiant dusks against which fleets of boats stand out like velvet.

I think of a string of enchanted evenings vividly remembered because unforgettable. I think of the deep blue of the sea one night at Pocasset, of the fresh and varied greens of the verdure ashore, of the trimness of the dwellings at Barlow's Landing, each as sharply etched as the vessels moored around us. I think of a sun setting as sumptuously over Buzzard's Bay as it does over the prairies (and gilding the masts and rigging of incoming yachts).

I think of Osterville—of how a perfect summer's day in a perfect Cape Cod port had been succeeded by an evening that was peacefulness itself. Apart from the plashing of fish—and the geese that dusk transformed into lustrous silhouettes—nothing had moved. Only the cheeping of birds had broken the stillness. Like the sky, the sea at that hour had been as bright as fire, yet limpid and cool. All the barriers that usually intrude between ourselves and our surroundings had seemed dissolved. In a mood akin to the mystic, we had felt a small but elated part of a great and harmonious whole.

I think of a glassy Tenant's Harbor and of its atmosphere of crystal after a long bout with fog. I think of an old scow there named *Muriel,* transfigured by the rays of a waning sun into an object of beaten gold. I think of a trio of buoys bejeweling the sea: winking red, flashing white, glowing green.

I think of an evening in our home port of Scituate that was a symphony in silver. Of another in Plymouth of a Chinese red; of yet another in Marblehead, as burnished a bronze as a Rembrandt painting. I think how Edgartown and Cuttyhunk have reminded us at times of little Mideastern villages set into the hills—so still have they lain under moon and stars.

I think of night's striking blacks and whites. How calm and bright and almost holy sailboats look beneath their masthead and anchor lights and with their stern lamps softly shining. How neat the sweep of a lighthouse beacon or of spotlights searching basins for a mooring! I think of harbor waters dark and smooth as marble; of towns whose tangle of lights twinkle like diamonds.

I think of the moon spangling the sea with silver as it rises in the east. I think of white moons and yellow moons; of twists of moons and moons huge and splendid slowly climbing over firs.

I think of the ferry *Uncatena* backing into her berth at Vineyard Haven, brilliantly lit and belching smoke, and suggesting nothing so much as a dance hall on fire, as her passengers crowd her opening as if eager to escape. I think of lightning forks as orange as pumpkins. Of canopies of color over the Fourth of July, bathing anchorages in extravagant hues.

I think of hosts of little boats skimming about like fireflies. Of behemoths all quiet engines and rich gold lamps. Of church spires dazzling as topazes; of running lights resembling rubies and emeralds.

I think how often evening itself is the experience. How life at sundown and after dark is less a matter of instinct or intellect—or even sympathy—but pure aesthetics. An enjoyment—as Joyce Cary once wrote about art—that has no relation with appetite or self-satisfaction. That is something freely given, "a good, a grace, belonging simply to existence, to reality itself."

On Rude Realities

MENTION BOATING TO A NONSAILOR AND THERE is an almost universal assumption of pleasure. The image conjured is one of blue skies, smooth seas, and your vessel cleaving the water like a poem. But practitioners of the sport know a ruder reality. Sixty percent of any season is inclement. And by inclement I mean the whole range of imperfect conditions from "glop" to nasty weather.

In combination or by themselves, the elements can run a disagreeable gamut. Anyone who has ever been caught in a squall or a gale would never doubt Geoffrey Scott's description of wind as "a fiend, Dark and wild." So furious are some of its blasts that even in your harbor there will be whitecaps, while at your mooring the surge will be such that you will have to close your eyes against the motion. If tempests are a part of cruising, so are doldrums, hour upon hour of no wind and no way when you seem to be marking time over the same piece of ocean. Temperatures, too, can embody extremes. Now as hot and terrible as the mistral, the wind can also be so chill and damp it will turn you to stone, almost, as you huddle, shivering, on a locker in the cockpit. To say nothing of the wind as a tease. "As soon seek roses in December, ice in June," Byron once wrote of the element, as "hope constancy" in the wind.

The sun is another Janus. Usually a blessing, it is responsible on occasion for abysmal headaches, for sores on your lips, for that knot behind the eyes that only sleep can relieve. After an eight- or nine-hour sail, the sun can seem like a laser beam boring into your temples. Its rays can toughen flesh to the texture of cardboard or sear it to the point where it feels as if it is just about to go up in smoke. Some of us go stupid with its heat. On sluggish days at sea with hardly a zephyr, our souls come to a full stop and we find it a challenge to put two coherent thoughts together. Indeed, so sensitive are we to "the eye of heaven" that we disappear for the summer behind dark glasses and under hats and an inch of protective ointment.

A third trial is motion. Not just the dismal rolling, pitching, and tossing encountered during foul weather (which condition once prompted Dr. Johnson to remark that "Being in a ship is being in a jail with the chance of being drowned"), but the sheer physical wear and tear of being constantly on the move. One can become weary of the need to brace, of lumpy seas and of rolly slips and anchorages (and particularly those after a rude passage). Many a sailor finds that his sense of balance is still bobbing long after a voyage is over. Not to mention tidal surge when cooking dinner—an aggravation every first mate would gladly forgo—along with those wakes that send utensils flying.

As immediate as the outer are the inner realities to be confronted. Where is the sailor whose spirit has never paled before a blow? Who has never experienced, in private at least, failures of nerve or of courage? Closely allied to fear is the anxiety that is more debilitating than *mal de mer*. In some, this apprehension isn't as to finalities like drowning or being sunk, but of discomfort and of somehow not measuring up to expectations. (Both those you fancy others are holding for you and, worse, those you are exacting of yourself.) Inertia is another dragon that must be slain on many a passage. Laziness, once surrendered to, can devolve into lassitude and lassitude into that impotence in which you simply take up space on a boat. And who among us is completely free of the pettiness engendered by the special strains of life afloat?

These and other miseries admitted, why then do we cruise?

No knowledgeable sailor views himself as a victim. To the best of his ability and control, he plays the weather. Wise in the ways of safety and comfort, he equips his vessel with the proper instruments and with stores suitable to cope with a variety of circumstances. Such a mariner never stops learning. Or striving for an active endurance when endure he must. Those rude realities that are sometimes thrust upon him are not, he has discovered, without their gifts—flexibility among them and the heady satisfaction when a challenge is met. Happier still is his command of a truth— that "on the starboard hand of every woe" (as Melville phrased it), "there is a sure delight; and higher the top of that delight, than the bottom of the woe is deep."

To one thus instructed, the "salt, inhospitable sea" is essentially sweet.

On an August Gale

"THE WEATHER BUREAU'S A DISGRACE!" WARREN blurted at noon. At 11:00 the Coast Guard, at least, had raised small-craft warnings, though the forerunning wind of the "front" (or whatever it was) had whacked us at 10:00.

Aboard our Sabre twenty-eight-foot sloop *Serena,* Warren and I had been underway since 7:00 A.M., hoping to make our home port of Scituate by early afternoon. A front with winds of fifteen to twenty-five knots and possible showers and thunderstorms had been predicted for late in the day, weather that we reckoned to beat home with time to spare.

Moored the night before in Pocasset, an anchorage at the northeast end of Buzzard's Bay, we had been treated to a glorious sunset—one of those flamboyant shows you associate with twilight in the tropics. Maybe, we had reasoned, the forecasters were wrong about tomorrow, which dawned with no "red skies" as "sailors' warnings."

Rather, it was gray and calm as we crossed the three-mile corner of the bay from Pocasset to the west end of the Cape Cod Canal. Even the Hog Island Channel, which can be horrendous on occasion, was utterly still. Notwithstanding that the National Oceanic and Atmospheric Administration was still forecasting the "front," we had elected to leave. All season we had been listening to virtually the same prediction. Indeed, where weather was concerned, it had been more a plague than a summer. Always and forever the same conditions: "hot, hazy, humid; southerly winds, variable, except in possible showers and thunderstorms, extending," as NOAA intoned with monotonous regularity, "right through the weekend." Now, after a two-week cruise of motoring all around Narragansett and Buzzard's Bays, in weather punctuated by squalls but otherwise so windless we hadn't raised a sail except for shade, we just wanted on this August Friday to get home.

The canal, too, was smooth and silvery, its

only disconcerting note a black sky hung like a dropcloth off in the west. Under its trio of bridges we powered; past green banks dappled with flowers and dotted with trailers and tents; by fishermen and figures on bicycles or on foot. "Nice of them to build this big ditch for us, wasn't it?" Warren remarked pleasantly as we motored along, enjoying the fresh scents from the water and the trees and the sounds of the birds twittering in early morning. Still . . . still . . . something in me was on the alert. I didn't trust this pacific passage or, rather, trusted its beneficence only as far as the Harbor of Refuge at the east end of the Canal. Taking turns at the tiller, the skipper and I donned our foul-weather gear before and not after the possible fact.

In respect to putting out into a weather unknown, sailors are perpetual pioneers. A given in boating is the transience of conditions. Though you do what you can to educate yourself about the elements, seldom are the forecast and the weather identical. Even the most cautious, methodical mariners get "caught out." When we cleared the canal at 8:30 we knew we had left shelter and were now out on our own on the ocean proper. Today, I kept reminding myself (to keep apprehension at bay), is right now, and right now wasn't so bad. In fact, we congratulated ourselves on encountering a Cape Cod Bay ruffled by only a slight chop under a southwest wind of fifteen knots.

To this point we had covered ten miles of a forty-mile passage (for the canal had added seven to the three already made). Thirty miles remained from the canal to Scituate—roughly a five-hour stint if we could maintain a speed of six knots. To this end we determined to "motorsail"—raising our main and 115 percent genoa for whatever "lift" and additional speed they could add to that of our Atomic Four gas engine. Because it was being backwinded by the main we soon dropped our headsail; and for the next ninety minutes—which brought us just past the Manomet whistler buoy—we watched the wind build slowly and steadily to twenty knots. Even so, if it steadied there, we reflected, and remained on the port quarter of our boat, we'd net ourselves a fairly pleasant passage home.

Wham! It struck like that, a west wind of thirty-five knots without warning and almost knocking us down. "Get down the main! Quick!" my husband exclaimed. I lumbered forward as fast as my cumbersome foul-weather gear would permit and hauled it down. "Take your time. Take your time," I whispered to myself, shaking a little—more from being startled than afraid—as I braced against the boom while I unscrewed the main's halyard shackle. "Unscrew it straight so it won't wedge stuck" (as it can at certain angles) I counseled myself. Naturally it jammed. "I can't do it!" I cried, aware before the words were out that I *had* to. "Of course you can," insisted the skipper encouragingly. Shutting the tumult out with a deliberate effort, I concentrated on the task. "Now for goodness' sake, don't let it go!" I warned myself, hanging on to the shackle for all I was worth as I ducked under a canvas flapping so rudely I hoped it wouldn't knock me overboard and took the shackle to the lifeline to secure it. Lose the main halyard in a wind like that and all kinds of disastrous mischief would result! "From now on," I pronounced, as I scrambled back to the shelter of the cockpit and took the helm so that Warren could furl and tie the main, "we're going to wear our harnesses when it blows up!"

At fifteen knots the sea starts to whitecap. Sixteen to nineteen, and you remark to each other that there's a lot of wind. Twenty to twenty-five, and you've entered the realm of drama. Twenty-six to thirty, and it's time, generally, for most prudent sailors to put into port. Every knot above thirty the wind becomes more wall-like while the sea is transformed from a liquid entity to one that seems hewn from quartz. Within minutes we were experiencing gusts to forty and then to forty-five and fifty and, almost in disbelief, had switched our anemometer to its highest gauge. In an hour and a half we had gone from a flat calm to a fresh gale.

Both of us thought back to our previous high-water mark of hazard—a mid-October passage several years before with another couple aboard their forty-eight-foot yawl en route from Nantucket to Falmouth. Then, too, we had been swamped by an unpredicted gale of comparable ferocity. Flying our heaviest jib and mizzen, with two men spelling each other at the wheel every quarter hour, rail under, we'd managed to hold one steep angle of heel for hours, just praying we wouldn't have to tack—or that a sail wouldn't tear, a shroud part, the mast break.

Now our sails were down and our concerns a bit different. Today we were alone and on a much smaller boat. We weren't beating as we had been on that other occasion, but motoring in the trough of seas that were soon eight to twelve feet—short, steep waves whose crests were being whipped into froth, and that were combed, alas, with the lobster pots that blanket this stretch of coast. Instead of a "dry front" with an almost arctic purity of visibility, the air was full of spume that clouded our glasses and stung our eyes. Above us ran a wolfpack of clouds; at our stern our Avon rubber dinghy grunted like a rooting pig. And all this savage, seething world was a sullen black, except for an eerie chartreuse where the ocean shallowed.

The only way out of such a malevolent situation is through it. Like David versus Goliath, it is your brains against the brawn and brutality of the sea. You snap to in danger, summoning not only the dumb, dogged patience needed to endure rude passages, but an absolute concentration. Tension is compressed into a thin little sheet and shoved somewhere deep in the gut to be expelled later in a torrent of chatter and luxurious relief. As always, the primary responsibility for our safety rested squarely on the skipper's skillful shoulders, but all my force marshaled itself into a helpful vigilance.

The last thing in the world we needed—after one of us going overboard—was to lose the use of our engine by having our propeller get hung up on the line of a lobster pot. And approaching the vicinity of Plymouth, there are so many! With barely a boat beam's worth of distance between them, it's like threading a needle to pick your way among them. Challenging at best, how much more difficult to avoid these menaces to navigation when the sea is boiling and hurling spray in your faces all the while. I finally removed for good the sunglasses that I wear perpetually at sea and kept wiping the skipper's regular glasses with the paper towels I had earlier wadded into my jacket pocket. Continually our two pairs of eyes raked the ocean in an effort to steer a meticulous course through this minefield of "watch" buoys. Shoulder-to-shoulder, soul-to-soul, teamed as we had been so many times before against the kind of conditions that Conrad once described as "ruthlessly frank"—charged with the same high pitch of perception—on we slogged: ducking spray, detecting and dodging pots, debating as time dragged by and we drew nearer the Gurnet, whether or not we ought to alter our destination.

Thirty miles can seem like three hundred on a turbulent ocean. By midday we'd come ten miles from the Canal with twenty left to get to Scituate.

The gale showed no signs of abating and the sea was still a cauldron. Was "the Devil we could see"—Plymouth—preferable to "the Devil we couldn't"—the rest of the voyage? Two years before a spring gale had registered seventy knots in these same waters—and this blast, we were aware, might do so again. Did it make any sense for *Serena* to continue?

Making Plymouth, we recognized, would be no picnic. Powering up its long, tricky, meandering channel we would have both the tide and wind against us, and seas, consequently, in these restricted waters, would be even higher and more confused than those offshore. Not to mention a million more pots to have to negotiate, some of which would be sunken. On balance, running that gauntlet seemed, nonetheless, the wiser option.

Our own safe passage into Plymouth engaged us necessarily, but we also kept an eye on the other yachts in the area sharing the travail. The weirdly fluttering boat way ahead. (What was it? Power or sail? We couldn't tell, even with the binoculars.) The small black sloop to port that had had so much trouble gathering in her flapping jib, and which sometimes sank from view right down to her boom. The handsome cream and maroon-colored ketch we'd seen earlier banging its way down to the canal, and which had now turned around, obviously thinking better of the passage. The passel of lobster and other boats hastening to port, the grave faces of their crews riveted now on the ocean, now on their craft, with only the tersest of nods and waves in passing. Each lonely vessel, like our own, cursing the weather bureau, no doubt, while contending with the elements as best it could.

The only silver lining in this cloud of storm was that it was warm. As we lumbered in the channel, going up one swell and down another (their tops smoking as foam was blown in streaks along the direction of the wind), we were drenched constantly. The atmosphere was far too thick with scud, I thought regretfully, to take a picture. All morning part of me had been reveling disinterestedly in the spectacle presented by the adverse. Had it been possible I would have loved to be a seagull hanging above it and feasting my yellow eye on the whole terrible sweep of the scene. Though I longed to record conditions with my camera, I didn't dare—for salt damages lenses. Nor was there time to dart below and take a shot from the relative calm of the cabin. We were too busy and the concentration too continuous to permit anything but the briefest general glances around us. Despite the fact that I knew that pictures can't convey the sound, smell, or feel of tempests—that even the hugest seas "flatten" out in photographs—with a feeling of loss I surrendered any idea of capturing this maelstrom on film.

Images, however, abounded. Rearing over the shoals inshore were waves as green as cobras. To starboard a dismasted yacht dragging three pots she had managed to snag was being towed in by a lobsterman.

Another boat, a cutter, had turned her stern to the "graybeards" that rose in ridge upon ridge, while her skipper studied the chart for what must have been to him an unfamiliar waterway. As *Serena* made a slow three knots up the channel, the windows in the dwellings atop the Gurnet seemed, like horrified eyes, to watch our wallowing, and that of a handful of other vessels, whose masts resembled pendulums as they swayed from side to side. And now commenced the cloudbursts that heretofore had held off, accompanied by thunder and lightning of a vivid orange and sulfur yellow.

Sometimes paradise is putting into port. Not

Plymouth that day. Even in the most protected part of the anchorage, the wind was blowing at thirty knots, and it was rougher on the mooring that we gratefully picked up at 1:00 than it is most times when we're underway. For hours — as we pitched and tossed and were pummeled by the rains that swept over in waves—our mast shook, our halyards beat furiously, our sail cover kept blowing off its restraining hooks (and had to be lashed). Above decks we could hardly hear each other when we spoke.

Below, we listened to fragments of dramas on our marine radio. "Cape Cod Canal Coast Guard! Cape Cod Canal Coast Guard!" yelled a frantic voice over channel 16. "How long is this going to last? We're gettin' beat up out here!"

"Do you need assistance, sir?" returned the calm voice of the Coast Guard. No reply. Transmitting over channel 22 were a commercial fishing boat and her spotter plane, *Yellowbird,* from Nova Scotia, the latter reporting that it had been flying in and out of thunderstorms all day. "Going to have to put into Plymouth," the plane determined. "No . . . we see clearing ahead may go on to Boston."

Then, nothing. "*Yellowbird?*" radioed the fishing boat repeatedly, "Click twice if you're receiving our messages." Nary a click came from the aircraft.

Safe ourselves, we were holding a good thought for all those yachtsmen still battling that mean wind and wild ocean. Throughout the afternoon, Plymouth Harbor became a magnet, sucking in almost every boat in a ten-mile radius, both power and sail, whether heading south or coming north. Even the "big babies," including some transatlantic sailors, were quitting Cape Cod and Massachusetts Bays this day. "Dat was bad out dere," commented a Dutch couple as they motored by, as surprised as everyone else by the vicious barrage.

Sailors pluck lessons from such elemental extremes. Subsequent to that junket we had a second set of reef points added to our main. We purchased a small, tough, "working" jib for storm conditions. (For what if our engine had failed? What sort of canvas would we have raised so as not to be overcanvased?) We also bought trim new life vests to replace our bulkier old-fashioned life jackets, to which we attached personal strobe lights in case of going overboard.

Arduous as our passage had been, it had boiled down to demanding piloting. With all our trials and uncertainties, we had ventured, on that August 11, only on the edge of risk. Others, less fortunate, were later to be plunged into its appalling substance. For unknown to us at the time, the wave disturbance that had assailed us aboard *Serena*—a low that had been born over the plains of Minnesota and then swept east—would next tear across the Atlantic, deepening and intensifying en route as it joined with another low—and then smash into the Fastnet fleet of three hundred and three boats racing seventy miles off the coast of England. In a span of twenty hours on the 13th and 14th of August, 1979, a Force 10, sixty-knot gale with forty- to fifty-foot breaking waves would capsize seventy-seven yachts, knock a hundred horizontal, and kill fifteen people.

"Experience," Thomas Hardy once wrote, "is as to intensity, not duration."

On Black Zero Fog

ANYONE WHO HAS CRUISED THE COAST OF Maine has a tale of fog to tell, and *Sea Story II* can add a chapter or two.

We were heading for the ninth time for the coast of Maine (previously explored by us in a variety of vessels, both power and sail).

Why another voyage Down East? From past experience we were well aware of the region's ledges and lobster pots; of its fabled fogs; that its water was colder; its distances longer; its facilities far fewer as you made your way east. We knew that anchoring in Maine can be a muddy mess; and that mosquitoes at dusk are an absolute blight.

But we were even more mindful of the magic that is Maine. Of its lavish forests of fir, so fragrant the entire coastline smells like Christmas. Of its bold, blue mountains and teal-colored sea. Of its seals and porpoises and sounding whales. Of its windjammers winging about. Of its complex of contrasts—from the remoteness of Roque through the stately shores of Mount Desert to the paradise of Pulpit Harbor (and of Merchants Row, each of whose myriad of islands is more idyllic than the next) to the beehive harbors of Boothbay and Camden, not to mention the port of Portland, as cosmopolitan as it is commercial.

This year, instead of our usual three weeks we had only two to spend and we left with the idea of a flexible itinerary. To date, we'd gone as far east as Grand Manan Island, New Brunswick, so we felt no pressure to make any particular port. Good thing, in the light—or rather, the lack of it—of what was to come.

After all the extensive preparations a cruise entails, your first day out you'd love to draw an "easy" day. Too often, you net just the reverse.

What we drew, as we departed our home port of Scituate on the last day of July—heading for Newcastle, New Hampshire, via the outside route around Cape Ann—was a windless, rather hazy day with a heavy easterly roll; conditions that lasted until shortly before we reached the Cape Ann whistler buoy. Streaming suddenly over the water from the east—and completely unpredicted—came a wall of mist that engulfed the boat and extinguished visibility. Grabbing the binoculars and the chart, down from the flybridge Warren and I hastened into our cabin and into our standard radar procedure. Setting the lower station autopilot, the skipper scanned the radar, which was already warmed up (a precaution we take on days when conditions are indefinite). With Warren monitoring the instruments, I cracked open the windshield the better to hear the buoy and whatever else might be around and peered at the sea ahead for pots and other hazards. Though we never saw them visually, we dodged around many small craft off Rockport that we spotted on the screen.

The pea-soup fog that had socked in stayed socked in, the heavy following swells built, with a southeast breeze astern as we crossed Bigelow Bight and went inside an unsighted Isles of Shoals in zero visibility. A speeding lobster boat, a large Jarvis Newman and *Sea Story II* arrived at the 2 KR whistler off Portsmouth, New Hampshire (which you couldn't see until you practically ran

into it), at the same time—making for an inter-
esting several minutes of maneuvering. Almost
instantly the Jarvis Newman, the lobster boat, and
the mark evaporated, leaving *Sea Story II* to crawl
for a mile on radar with a strong ebb current to
the Little Harbor breakwater area.

The first mate was now up on the bow trying
to find can number one, which turned out to be
what seemed an enormous green tower of a day
marker looming up to port with surf breaking on
ledges too close for our comfort behind. Mean-
time the skipper was doing his best to avoid a
number of pots even harder to discern because
of current and surf while monitoring a radar
now a jumble of land returns. Somehow *Sea
Story II* and the chase boat sent out by the Went-
worth Marina to lead in its transients found each
other in the fog with the help of radio communications and the honking of horns. A real dry-
mouth passage of labor and challenge had thus
initiated our journey.

The next day was to hold another unexpected
event.

There are certain givens to any cruise to Maine.
You know you're going to see plenty of cormorants, kayaks, and Cruising Club of America

yachts. You know you're going to roll in the ports of Camden, Port Clyde, Bar Harbor, and Roque —and in the Gulf of Maine, which is rolly as a rule not an exception. Just as it was this day, though only moderately so as we headed for Boothbay Harbor in cool, sunny conditions making about ten and a half knots as we bucked a half-knot current. Just past Seguin and with about three miles to go to bell number one off the Cuckolds, we were reminded of yet another given—that Maine can go down in a minute.

There is no element more deceptive as to size, sound or distance than fog—or more dangerous. If you're going buoy-to-buoy in the mire so is everybody else, so traffic itself becomes a problem. Warren and I had just commented to each other that we only had about a two-mile cone, when the large blue sailboat to our starboard and somewhat ahead abruptly vaporized. That—and a sudden eerie paling of the light like that of an eclipse— sent us scurrying back down into the cabin an instant before *Sea Story II* was swamped. With no cone at all—let alone twenty feet, two hundred feet, or two miles—we reduced speed to five and a half knots and nosed toward Boothbay on full radar and loran navigation. Intermittently, sailboats appeared and disappeared, close aboard, just ahead, astern; some in company, some by themselves, but all suggesting phantom fish glimmering in the dimness of the deeps. Now and then you'd glimpse the golden twinkle of a radar reflector high up in the murk (but nothing else); or you'd hear the tinny hoot of an airhorn. Periodically we'd sound our own loud blasts; with every crew grateful, you may be sure, for the steady hoots from the Cuckolds and the horn on Burnt Island as each vessel felt its cautious way from mark to mark.

Nice as are the ports of York and Kennebunkport, this crew never feels as if we're really in Maine until we pass Old Anthony, the buoy off Cape Elizabeth. Similarly, the "Country of the Pointed Firs" is best embodied for us as we enter Boothbay Harbor—usually so sparkling, wide, and wonderful an anchorage that we almost hear trumpets as we approach.

As we crept in on this occasion—with the exception of the briefest of scale-ups when Squirrel Island was abeam and then at red #4— we saw nothing until we rounded McKown Point and motored into the basin of the Boothbay Harbor Yacht Club.

A mooring at the yacht club is the best berth in the harbor in our opinion—sheltered, quiet, with launch service and a trim facility at your disposal and scenic walks in both directions if you don't mind hills. When you can see them there are also a laboratory, a Coast Guard base, and handsome condominiums and houses on its bordering shores, as well as a view of a good deal of the harbor.

As much as as possible we cruise not to endure but to enjoy, so we elect not to put out into zero if we don't have to. In the two and a half days we were to be pinned down in Boothbay, we availed ourselves of many a stroll ashore. We also ran the engine at the mooring for a period each day to charge the batteries; and when the veil lifted in the inner harbor for a spell, we'd motor around its docks and downtown areas. We'd watch the lobstermen who'd materialize to pull their pots without a wasted minute or motion; and downed our drinks during "happy hours" inside the cabin due to the damp and the chill.

Once, we attempted a departure early in the morning only to run smack into the shroud at Squirrel Island. Doing a 180 to "wait and see" we returned to the yacht club and picked up its out-

ermost mooring to better scan conditions—and
remained there, listening to "Securitie" calls for
the rest of the day.

Mostly we were absorbed in the arts and wiles
of fog—fog receding seaward only to roll back
in; fog sifting off the encircling hills; fog in dol-
lops and billows and balls, in sheets and swatches
and rills; fog as tyrant and fog as tease.

A strange tangerine sun was dropping shafts
through holes in the heaped-up clouds, infusing
the sea with a light orange glitter when *Sea Story
II* departed Boothbay Harbor bound for Tenant's.
We were going the "outside route," electing to
skip the ports of Muscongus Bay.

If you're rarely out of sight of a lobster boat
Down East—whose scores form a sort of unoffi-
cial safety net should you develop a problem—you
are taxed mightily for the dividend. Much of
Maine looks as if a bag of confetti had been
dumped on its waters, so numerous are its lobster
pots and buoys, which extend to several miles offshore. But add the menace of "watch buoys" or
"toggles," as they are sometimes called, with lines
that can extend twenty feet or more from the pot
buoy, and you literally have a minefield for the
transient pleasure cruiser. And this plethora of

pots—more lethal than ledges or fog—seems to proliferate by the season. In the Boothbay Harbor we had just exited, there are so many pot buoys among the moorings that parts of the port look like a pincushion. No locale is worse in this regard than Muscongus Bay, and we have long since wearied of its "Watch-for-the-watch-buoys" fun and games.

When we left Boothbay at 7:00 we had about one mile of visibility and were grateful even for that limited scope. This lowered to a quarter mile at the Hypocrite Ledge midchannel bell in Fisherman's Passage, but lifted somewhat off Muscongus, where we passed a few stray sailboats pasted in the haze. The hood was once again pulled over our heads when we were just a couple of miles from the Old Man Ledge whistler. A monstrous tidal wave of fog to starboard—seemingly stationary and dark as any squall (nervously eyed by the first mate all the while)—broke over our boat.

Boating has its benchmark experiences: the worst head sea, the worst following sea, the highest winds, the most miles made in a day. There are also kinds and qualities of fog. There are white fogs, gray fogs, lurid fogs, luminous fogs—

this one was black zero fog without a trace of light, the dirtiest fog we've ever been called upon to navigate. High adventure is inherent in such a fog. To use every ounce of yourself every instant for hours on end is a living of life on the edge and is exhausting, even when your vessel is equipped with all the electronics. Running strictly on instruments, the skipper himself becomes an instrument interpreting instruments. You have no past or future—only the concentrated and perilous present.

Back up on the bow went the first mate to be met by two waves' worth of visibility with an occasional seagull skimming over the tops of the swells. For an instant I was tired of being a grown-up grown-up doing the best she could for as long as she could and wished I were a seagull, free of the task of having to help find our way into safe harbor. With a face full of cold fog and without my fog-filtering sunglasses (too continuously misted up to bother with), I became a pair of vigilant eyes raking the bit of sea ahead and a pair of ears straining to hear Old Man whistling.

Even with the aid of radar and loran, to actually sight the buoy visually in zero visibility is like searching for a needle in a haystack. Far from resembling a needle when you find it, the mark is apt to loom up suddenly as a ghostly apparition, like some giant Egyptian mummy or a "haunt." After the Old Man had been found we crept along dodging craft we never saw up to the Marshall Point red-and-white whistler, which emerged when we could just about touch it. Next, the skipper set his course for green bell #1 off Southern Island outside of Tenant's Harbor, a distance of 2.2 miles. Proceeding at dead slow—with the windshield open to hear the first mate's reports of pots ahead—Warren maneuvered, alternating both shafts to avoid the "tide-running multitude" of lobster pot buoys in a dark that was truly Stygian. Eventually we reached bell #1 by radar, of course, but also by its sound, sighting it at a yard or two to port.

Another malicious network of pots exists around and within Tenant's Harbor. The skipper was to perform a first-rate feat of seamanship as he threaded an absolutely diabolical gauntlet of them. In a netherworld of nothingness, going all-slow and on full radar to enter harbor; dodging pots to port, to starboard, dead ahead, and sometimes all at once—backing—gliding in neutral—one shaft and then another—trying to average a radar heading, he steered manually to go up through what eventually became the indistinct blobs of dozens of moored and anchored boats.

The first obscure image to appear was a huge schooner rising up like a specter ship out of the "Ancient Mariner" just slightly left and ahead. "Are you in the harbor?" I shouted to the wraith on its bow—whose reassuring reply was that he was at anchor and the first boat inside the mouth. Then other barely discernible vessels suggested themselves in the blackness, their crews peering at the crew of *Sea Story II* like shades from some mythical underworld. Indeed we might as well have been in Hades as we picked up the first mooring with a pickup buoy we encountered and switched off the engine. "Great boat, great instruments, great teamwork!" cried the skipper as, exuberant with relief, we threw our arms around each other and hugged each other tight.

For twenty-four more hours Tenant's remained swaddled. Its considerable fleet, which included many yachts from the Blue Water Cruising Club, would periodically emerge and then vanish in the vagaries of fog, which mostly was dense. (So thick, in fact, that the skipper set a compass course to row to shore.) Scanning our VHF radio, we knew that mariners all up and down the coast from Cutler to Casco Bay had to cope with the frustration of enforced inactivity. Some, balancing their restiveness against the risks, chose to depart Tenant's, a decision we thought unwise after the foulness we had just transited.

Warren used this interlude to draw courses into every harbor we might possibly enter hereafter, not just to their entrance buoys.

Now commenced a blessed respite of several days. Cheered by blue skies, smooth seas, and a light westerly, everybody who could set a sail or start an engine quit Tenant's in what amounted to a mass exodus.

When the weather is fair there is no finer sojourn than the fifty-mile run we now made from Tenant's Harbor to Mount Desert. Indeed it was a cruise through calendar and postcard country.

Much of the best of Maine is encompassed by such a junket—its beautiful bays—the west and east Penobscot, Jericho, and Blue Hill; two straits as near divine as waterways can be—the Fox Islands and Deer Isles Thorofares; not to mention the Muscle Ridge Channel, Casco Passage, the Bass Harbor Bar—or the splendid sweep of Western Way leading up to Mount Desert and

Southwest Harbor for *Sea Story II* and Hinckley's new marina. En route, the staunch poetry of a string of lighthouses; a plenitude of firs (each water-sculpted slab of rock crammed with its own flawless stand); neat dwellings tucked into nests of clouds or set, as in Stonington, into the sides of hills; pull boats from Outward Bound adding to your sense of sailing in the last century (despite your modern yacht); and all along a coast in which the wild and the domesticated exist in an almost perfect meld.

Next day, because of time constraints, we reversed the reel and returned to Tenant's, not willing to chance that fog might yet again descend and trap us this far east. And the day after that we ran more westward still to Robinhood in visibility that allowed us to see Old Man and all that company of other aids we'd lately sweated blood to find.

Robinhood, alas, reverted and we wakened our first morning there to a world without features. Sporadically the fog would shrink, but only enough to leave us sitting in a bowl of blue surrounded by glop.

"Too bad we're not a helicopter," the skipper muttered disgustedly as we moved from slip to mooring to slip again waiting on the will of the fog. Twice our efforts to leave were repulsed by a tent of white vapor as wide as the river and running the length of the Sheepscot, our course out to sea. Scanning the VHF radio (a source that was proving more reliable than the NOAA, which had never forecast fog), we learned that most of the rest of the coast had likewise been swallowed.

When a horizon produced itself we scooted to Portland and more of the "now-you-see-Maine, now-you-don't" syndrome. Midmorning of our second day when the fog finally scaled to "patchy," we hightailed it to Newcastle, but not without another shutdown en route.

"It'll be a long time before I con our good ship back to Maine," the skipper pronounced as we pulled into Scituate, after a leg not unlike our first day out—the wind never having come up enough to permanently peel away the drear. Remembering the spicy breath of spruce; the shadows draped like dark scarves over the mountains of Mount Desert; three shining mornings of sharp horizons—the magic!—I knew that it would *not*.

On the Sublime

IRONICALLY, WHEN I WAS A POWERBOATER AND one who, in the main, preferred to cruise alone with her family, my two most memorable boating experiences had to do with sailboats and yacht-club cruises. Both occurred the same summer.

Finding ourselves temporarily boatless, my husband and I didn't have to be asked twice when a friend and his wife invited us to join them on their forty-three-foot yawl for the Boston Yacht Club's annual cruise in July. For me the pleasure would be threefold: Not only would I be cruising again, I would be cruising to Maine, my favorite cruising ground, and I would be cruising on a sailboat (something I had always wanted to do and never yet done). Nothing in powerboating had prepared me for the sensation of sailing. After motoring out of York Harbor on an idyllic morning (the first day had been not only bleak but windless, necessitating our motoring all the way from Marblehead to York)—the sails were set and the engine cut. The peace—the profound soundlessness—the easy gliding through the water under a twelve-knot westerly were almost unearthly. As I sat on the bow in the cool of the headsail, listening to its silky swish and to the foam steaming off the tumblehome, I felt as if the thirteen-ton vessel beneath me were nothing but a bit of thistledown. And I understood that for grace and beauty, minutes like this—except by their like—couldn't be matched in boating.

The second happened about a month later. After driving to a Power Squadron Rendezvous in Pocasset, a harbor at the northeast end of Buzzard's Bay, we joined another friend and his wife (this time on a cabin cruiser) for a tour of the harbor and its environs. It was an immaculate evening, with visibility as sharp and colors as deep and clear as they would be in October. About 6:00 the four of us on the flybridge looked out of Wings Neck Passage across miles of clear blue sea, and there—on a horizon precise as a course line—was a veritable army of spinnakers marching majestically up Buzzard's Bay toward Cleveland Ledge Light. It was the elite fleet itself, the sailing squadron of the mighty New York Yacht Club completing a day and a race on their annual cruise. We went out to meet them and reached the finish line by a buoy and committee boat beyond the lighthouse after about twenty percent of the fleet had swept over and were dropping their chutes. On and on they came— eighty-seven of the finest cruising and racing boats in America—all in a rainbow of hulls and spinnakers, with the sun and wind behind them (and us with no camera!). We turned at the end of the fleet and for four miles wended our way up through them as they headed for Pocasset anchorages—bagging sails, starting engines, hoisting drinks. We had the binoculars on the transoms as we came up on each group. Many of the Bermuda Race Group were there: the (then) radical new *Equation—Dove—Gem*—the beautiful blue sloop *Kato*. Stanley Rosenfeld was weaving in and out with his famous little *Foto* snapping pictures. As we approached the head of the fleet—the big boats that had finished in the first ten out of this huge armada—we came upon the famous *Windigo*—beside her the great *Bacarra*—beside her the black-hulled yawl *Inverness,* gold letters gracing her transom.

All of us were stirred to our depths. To be among them as they moved en masse was to be included, we knew, in something glorious. If there is a heaven, I thought, it must be something like your first sail or a once-in-a-lifetime encounter under perfect conditions with an elite fleet under spinnakers.

On the Wind in the Rigging

SAILING WE EQUATE WITH QUIET—AND TRANQUIL it often is. That instant when power is cut and the sails swell full, when waters at the bow "fold back, like earth against the plow," is as peaceful as the passage of an "angel's tear," falling, as Keats once put it, "through the clear ether silently."

In reality, however, even that calm is full of sound. Besides the slosh of wave, the sough of wind, the gurgle of water running out at the scuppers, there are the whistles and bells of the buoys that you pass; the buzz of lobster boats out pulling pots (which "plop" when cast back into the deep); the "thunk" of speedboats smacking the sea. Rattling from side to side in a cockpit pocket, your bilge pump handle "plonks" when you heel (accompanied in the cabin by the "clinking" of dishes). Not forgetting in fog the blasting of horns, or the dit-da-dit-da-dit of your loran.

At your yacht yard in March, the high whine of sanders slices the silence. Seagulls croak, moan, screech, and squawk as they wheel overhead. Canvases flap. "If I'd known it was going to be this warm," remarks a sailor working on the vessel next to your own, "I'd have left my long undies at home!"

A creaking in your mast disturbs you on your mooring. Or—"darumph, darumph"—your mooring buoy bumps your hull. Above, a plane drones over. Around you halyards slap, click, tinkle, and chink (or beat furiously during a blow). While airhorns hoot and toot for a launch—which promptly arrives with a swish and rumble—mains are dropped with a clank and a "whoosh." To say nothing of Lasers and catamarans "whisking" by with the speed of light.

Engines, you perceive, have their own refrains. Some cough and sputter when starting up; others fire with a guttural rush. A tinny rattle characterizes certain outboards; a putt-putt-putting some of the diesels. (Or else a steady reassuring churn.)

Yet another medley is audible from shore. A town whistle signals noon. Also by day, a yacht-club loudspeaker announces a phone call; a retriever barks for a ball to be tossed. The irritating revving of a mini-bike is matched after dark by the racing of drag cars. If concerts issue on Saturday nights from a bandstand in a parking lot, the Fourth erupts in fireworks, crowning a carnival's tuneful commerce.

Soothing—the plash of oars, the "plunk" of fish, the elegant thunder of pounding surf. In this port, a church clock chimes the hour. In that, the "bass eternal" of the sea is sounded in the deep honk and solid hum of a ferry. Not that all of your cruising is lyric. Here, a derrick whirrs and squeals while working on a jetty. There, small craft zip about like so many gnats. Or a bullhorn barks, a siren peals (aboard a Coast Guard cutter speeding out), rock music blares from an anchored boat.

More disturbing than clamor is a lack of sound. In fog, a passing seagull seems to be winging his way through velvet. As eerily silent, a crate moves by in the sea. And stillness when absolute can be downright oppressive, making you yearn, almost, for tempest and tumult.

But never for the sounds of the end of summer. For the "splat" of water hitting hardtop (as you flush out the cooling system of your now cradled vessel); for the "spurt" of oil being sucked from the engine; for the "splash" of antifreeze being poured into the bilge. Nor for the sighs and the sad pronouncement:

"Season's over. Time to go home."

On Our First Home Port

LIKE YOUR FIRST KISS, YOUR FIRST DATE—YOUR first *boat!*—your first home port has a special place in recollection. Our first marina was located up an estuary of the North River (New Inlet on the charts) in Scituate. Surrounding the river, as a setting might a jewel, was a marshland. No marriage in nature could be more felicitous. Not only was the former pretty and unpolluted (reputedly one of the few rivers left so in the state), the latter —from stubbled wastes through the summer when it resembled vast fields of green wheat to the autumn that bathed it in copper and rouge— was also poetic, an unfailing delight to the eyes and soul.

Our yacht yard itself, set neatly at its edge, was

Yankee in spirit. Here were found no tennis
courts, no swimming pool, no elaborate social calendar; nothing, in short, but good slips, fuel
pumps, a large "barn" for storage, and a mechanic
or two. For some yachtsmen the hustle-bustle of a
busy harbor is a necessity. Gregarious by nature,
their deepest needs are for an almost constant
activity and the company of other people. But we
(and especially me, I admit it) cherished our priva-
cy as boaters, and thus were more at home in an
atmosphere that allowed for solitude, should you
wish it.

One of the first things we noticed upon our
arrival was the stage of the tide. So high sometimes that it swamped its channels and flooded the
marsh, it was so low at others that the North
River became a sort of mini Colorado with steep,
canyonlike banks.

That the latter was treacherous we knew.
Narrow and winding, with a depth ranging from
three feet to eight feet, it was a maze of mud banks,
mussel beds, and sandbars ever shifting. Its real
menace, however, was its mouth. Shallow there
because of a bar, when wind and tide were opposing it could be furious. Waves of ten feet were not
uncommon, to say nothing of a current that

could almost match their height in knots (and bury your buoys to boot!). Over the years many boats had been wrecked and lives lost here. Yet on an average day in summer it was as busy as a canvas by Brueghel. Boaters, bathers, and beachcombers abounded. So did many a canine chasing gulls. (All on its spit.) Every inch of abutting water was accounted for by a boat. For what sand! What clear, invigorating water! What a view of the sea (there, in the distance, correct and stiff as a marine painting, but much ruder when you reached it, even when smooth). And fish enough to warrant your lashing a plastic rubbish barrel to the back of the deck.

For elegance—and a sense of peace and plenty—nothing can surpass a passage down this river. Grasses first, so close on either side you feel you could touch them, and lushness itself (or grace, as they bend into and then out of the wash of your boat). Then weather: azure today, or tonic or spanking or dour or foggy—with sometimes a scale-up that is highly dramatic. And birds everywhere: terns, coots, herons, gulls—here and there a red-winged blackbird sparking the marsh or an egret, sufficient—apparently—unto himself. And slim little beaches like crescent moons, dotted with clammers. Here's a lobster pot that's useless and dark as peat—there's a log—or stranded boat—or a single mast (and nothing else) moving along, as if on a canal through the flatness of Holland. The sharp crack and report of a gun: a puff of smoke. Hunters—with whom we are *not* in sympathy. And then a cliff all grand in the sun—three nuns (a bell buoy is spotted farther out)—white water, all around you swirling and frothing—a temperature drop—and out into the open sea.

Satisfying in every season, autumn was the time when we most deeply relished the river. As if by decree one molten weekend followed another in September. The sun had lost its intensity by then but not its warmth, and seemed intent on nothing but beneficence. Along with the worst of the heat had gone most of the haze, leaving colors and conditions that were absolute. Traffic, too, had diminished. (That these were the finest days of the year we had no doubt.) Beginning as blessing, October evolved into an assault. The marshes went yellow—as butter, as gold, as the fields at Arles; and the river turned so dark a blue as to appear malevolent. Like the "whetted knife" of Masefield's poem, the wind was cruel. Horizons, too, were brutal. By November 1 (which was when we were hauled) no one was left, or almost. There were the lobstermen still, and the clammers—no fair-weather souls they!—and an occasional diehard like ourselves. But beyond these nothing but gulls and marsh—bleak miles of it—wan, now, as corn with all its color gone. And just as beautiful.

On Dinghyology

You can't live with 'em; you can't live without 'em. Men? Women? No—dinghies.

Of every description from Boston Whalers down to makeshift rafts, dinghies—whether purchased or built by their owners; whether fashioned of fiberglass, rubber, or wood; whether inflatable or solid; whether sailing or nonsailing; whether cherished or derelict—are a whole experience unto themselves. There are dinghies shaped like dooughnuts, like saucers, like tubs; high-sided dinghies and dinghies with about an inch of freeboard.

Some dinghies are stowed on board—on the bow, on the stern, on the top of the cabin (or left collapsed and folded in their bags). Others are attached on davits to transoms. Or towed up close or trailing behind. Dinghies are encountered at dink docks, hauled up on shores, tied to pilings or to the ladders at certain piers (like the one at Provincetown, where one Zodiac, whose skipper hadn't allowed for the dropping of the tide, whipped around in gusty breezes like a kite!).

Dinghies can mean worry and care. They must be pulled in or let out. Affixed to your mooring when you don't choose to tow them. They must be outfitted with oars and/or engine. Must be cleaned and scraped. Caulked. Sanded. Varnished. Painted. Pumped up. Deflated. Since dinghies can be damaged by accident or intent (our Avon was slashed one night by vandals); can get lost or be stolen; can leak, swamp, or sink; can become untied and drift away or be flipped by high winds—they must be repaired, rescued, replaced. Now and then the engine of your dinghy won't fire, or eelgrass will foul its propeller. Or you'll get soaked in your tender, or broil or freeze. Or have to row against a gale of forty knots.

If a nuisance on occasion, dinghies are also employed for a host of happy purposes. From infants to ladies of advanced age clambering gamely into prams, they are used for transport.

They serve as ferries for guests and pets, not to mention provisions. As platforms for swimming, skin-diving, bathing. (Though there is certainly no graceful way to get into an inflatable after such a dunking. Half mermaid, half walrus, you heave yourself aboard any old way you can.) Dinghies are utilized for expeditions of exploration, of communication (in harbors when marine radios aren't being monitored), of investigation (when docks are full and you can't tie your boat up even briefly to ascertain what moorings are available). They run errands of mercy or recovery (including other people's "overboard" property).

Abetting in the letting off of steam (both physical and psychic) is another of their functions. Dinghies can be rowed in races among the youngfry; they provide adolescents with the means of escape for more sophisticated revelry ashore; allow their elders to get off by themselves—to fish, perhaps, or tour or just enjoy a breather. Dinghies make an ideal seat to clean your hull. And even protect it once in a while (as did our Avon one summer, "fending" our sloop from another that missed its mooring approach during something of a blow).

Yacht and dinghy appellations prove one of the most charming incidental pleasures of cruising. Many pairings—among them *Laughing Gull* and *Giggle, Goldenrod* and *Sneezy, My Harem* and *No Buoys*—are fetching. Still more are natural associations: *Vivacity* and *Frolic, Scylla* and *Charybdis, Zephyr* and *Puff*. If opposites like *Rich Al* and *Poor Dick, Liberation* and *Shackles,* and *Lonesome Traveler* and *Company* abound, so do variations on the theme of large and small—*Scallop* and *Scallopini, Sugar Daddy* and *Sugar Baby, Alley Cat* and *Kitten.* Some combinations play on a word or words—*Viewpoint* and *Point of View* for instance, or *Lady Lil* and *Lil Lady.* Others make music—*Songbird* and *Sea Note;* or evoke the dance—*Ballerina* and *Tutu;* or flights of a more literal order—*Wing and Wing* and *Feather.* Not forgetting the puckish *April Fool* and *Foolproof,* or that random, puzzling one-of-a-kind: *Pibroch* and *Chortle.*

Boon and curse. Trial and blessing. Saddled with; limited without. What else but our beloved dinghies?

On the Captain and Crew

OURS IS ALMOST THE ARCHETYPAL CAPTAIN. IN my husband a profound and lifelong love for the sea is matched only by deep respect. On a cruise, he leaves nothing to chance *but* chance. His chart work is thorough, his navigation careful, his investigation of any area we will be cruising to as complete as it can be. (The yachtsman who neglects to do his homework often sees the crown, he knows, without the jewels.) While his interest in the water is organic, in common with most other mariners (whether "ragmen" or "stinkpotters"), his need is for challenges that are concrete and physical.

Sources of pride to this sailor are a perfect piece of docking (he is the first one to lend a hand to other boaters when an approach is obviously difficult); being right "on" a buoy (which loran makes easy these days!); a tricky passage or new (to him) body of water that has been well executed. Sensible but not overly cautious—and ever mindful that you're never *there* where concentration is concerned, that the sea can not only bludgeon but charm you (like Circe) right into catastrophe—he never ventures out foolishly, but neither does he timidly hold back. (His instincts as to when to ignore or believe a forecast seem to us remarkably sure.) Above all he is human. He loves a boat show, boating talk, boating people. The arrival of any of his boating periodicals (he subscribes to them all) can make the dullest day special. Whether we're underway, anchored, moored, or snubbed to a slip; whether he's actively working or relaxing after effort, like Water Rat in *The Wind in the Willows,* my husband is never so happily employed as when "messing about" in a boat.

As a young family, our crew was always our children. We believe that boating brought us closer as a family. Together we experienced a whole spectrum of pleasures and pressures: rough waters and smooth, fair days and foul, good passages and bad. Together we went sightseeing, beachcombing, shopping, or dining out (something we were always meaning to do but never seemed to get around to in our immediate lives). Too absorbed in them at the time to have assessed their experiences, our children were richer than they knew. They stood on the top of Maine's Cadillac Mountain; and passed humbly in Plymouth through the *Mayflower*'s hold. At Mystic they gazed through a telescope; and sat in an old theater on Martha's Vineyard chuckling over a movie about Charlie Brown. Too closely closeted for too long, their emotions occasionally exploded; wide vistas made their spirits as spacious as themselves.

Their knowledge of the world of people was also expanded: from the venal (like the restaurateur on Cape Cod who grossly overcharged our son for the clams he needed for bait) to the host of genial slipmates and their offspring who added an easy substance and delight to cruising. They fed geese in Cataumet, gulls off a restaurant veranda in Nantucket, ducks in Scituate; they swam in pools, ports, and off the boat. Boating provided them both with some much-needed responsibilities. Among its gifts to our daughter, who always loved "to help," was the chance to contribute by doing dishes, by picking up the cabin, by fetching cold drinks for the captain and crew. Not to mention countless hours of fun—which, in the case of our son, was equated with fishing. A partial tally of the fish he caught on one of our vacation cruises included five mackerel, five flounder, seven scup, two eels, twenty seaperch, four herring, and two blowfish, a record that confirmed our feeling that with an angler like that in the family we'd never starve.

If an earlier enthusiasm for cruising with their parents gave way in their teens to a need to be with their peers (and properly so, though the latter were included, of course, whenever possible), our children knew that they were free to come back to boating, or not, as they chose. As for us—who can recall them (at Mystic) shinnying up anchors and cannons, or curled up in their V-bunks reading or drawing or dividing their "spoils," or sitting together on the bow, heads close (one in a dark blue Red Sox cap, the other in a white sailor, beneath which tumbled a long ponytail of wheat-colored curls)—"when we grow too old to cruise" —to paraphrase a tune from our youth—we'll have these to remember.

On Salty Dogs

POODLES MAKE GOOD SAILORS. SO DO LABRADOR and golden retrievers, and surprisingly—dachshunds. One of the most charming members of the latter pedigree (among our cruising acquaintances) was an old female named Heidi, who had to have the word B-O-A-T spelled in her presence, so excited did she become at the thought of her coming voyage. A springer spaniel was another enthusiast who won the hearts and admiration of all who were along on a recent yacht-club cruise. What a sight this pooch presented on his periodic sojourns ashore, perched in the bow of his dinghy, forepaws braced on the gunwales, back erect and ears blowing in the wind—as good a mariner (we believe) as Christopher Columbus or Captain Cook.

"Seasoned sailors" are what you'd dub a host of other canines we've scratched around with on the water. Herman, for instance, a schnauzer who lived aboard a fifty-three-foot motorsailer, and who had cruised the East Coast as far south as the Bahamas; and Buffy, half schnauzer, half who-knew-what? (and resembling nothing so much as a little buff-colored sheep), who enjoyed an annual two-week cruise each July to the islands of Martha's Vineyard and Nantucket. Buffy was also versed in the delights of both power and sail, zipping about her home port of Scituate, in a sailing dinghy with her master, when not aboard his motor vessel or larger sailing sloop. Not to mention Peek-a-Buoy, half Pekingese, half Airedale (but all heart!) whose maiden voyage on a twenty-six-foot auxiliary sailboat consisted of an odyssey from New Jersey to Nantucket and back.

When not pursuing rabbits, a beagle named Barney accompanied his owners on frequent fishing expeditions; while Borracho, a mutt of uncommonly good sea legs and fine manners was most gladdened by the "happy hour" repast enjoyed by his family and himself in whatever harbor they happened to drop hook. (Bring out the cheese and crackers and Borracho would sit up and roll over—along with licking his chops!) One of the most aristocratic of the "boaters" we've sniffed out was Bisquit, berthed in Rockland, Maine (and in the arms of his young mistress), a wheaten terrier who was not only nonshedding, but nonallergic. And surely Jamie, a black Lab owned by a launch driver for a yacht club, was the friendliest pup, wagging a "hello" or a "goodbye" to every passenger, as he spent the workday patrolling the decks in company with his steward.

These and other doggies heel, beat, reach, and run with the best of yachtsmen, or mush and bang, pitch and toss, rock and roll in the heaviest of seas. Their only "pet peeve" is being left aboard when all their human crewmates have journeyed ashore. As befits the species, their protest is vocal. (Many a croon, howl, and whine is heard in many an anchorage from many a mooring over the season.)

On vessels large and small, power or sail, pleasure or workboat, these "salty" dogs are otherwise cheerful, uncritical, and affectionate. To them and every other breed that braves the briny deep we say: "Fair winds!" And "Bone-voyage!"

On Autumn Sailing

THOUGH BOATING IS PLEASANT IN EVERY SEASON, an air of holiday pervades it in September. Banished with the heat of summer, with the murk that all too often shrouded the coast, with the midges and mosquitoes, with the sudden squalls, is that stagnant, tacky quality to the atmosphere that made you vaguely grumpy.

Distilled of all impurities, these days at sea are the true sparklers of the year. Since no one is off cruising, everyone is out sailing, their canvases crowding harbors and the waters beyond. (You will see more boats outside your home port on any weekend in September than at the height of summer.) In the clear air and crisp temperatures, a simple daysail has all the glamour of a voyage to

Spain. Adding to your sense of romance are freighters, rising on the horizon like medieval fortresses. Not to mention the mellow sun of the month or its majesty of color.

There is a blue special to September—a dark, sapphire blue, at once splendid and austere. This spartan blue—against whose depth of color boats seem cut from stiff white paper—is counterpoint to all the riotous foliage ashore. Without experience of it, autumn can't be fathomed to the full. Here, the mariner has the advantage of the landlubber; for not only is the sky above him blue, so is the sea on which he sails, the shore from which he embarks and to which he returns, which is bathed at this time of year in a luminous haze.

There is also less pressure on the sailor in September.

Inbuilt in every daytrip prior to your two-week summer cruise is the feeling that nice as *this* is, what's to come will be better still. By Labor Day that tension of expectation has been dispelled. Gone, too, are other summer strains: worry over the weather or getting a mooring or slip, concern over cruising your way through a body of water for the first time, anxiety over offspring left at home. However homely or brief, each cruise in autumn is what all cruises ought to be—an end in itself. Now is the time you're most apt to share your boat with guests (since people tend to scatter in the summer). Hanging on your mooring after such a sojourn, soaking up the delicious sun while enjoying a picnic lunch and conversation with relatives and friends is surely one of the best reasons for owning a boat.

If September is of the stuff of idyll, October proves more fickle and ascetic. Brisk little sea breezes are suddenly rude blasts; starchy little fair-weather clouds an ominous scud. There is still beatific weather to be savored, and blue-ribbon sailing, but in a day here or there, instead of halcyon stretches. By the middle of the month an icy wind is blowing out of the north. Lines that have been pliant all summer go chill and stiff. Even the sun feels cold. In a visibility that's absolute (and almost Arctic in its purity), seas of royal blue darken to purple.

For weeks you have been grateful for sweaters and heavy jackets, for mittens and woolen caps. (And for *soup* with your sandwich.) On occasion you have slept fully clothed, burrowed deep in a sleeping bag covered with a blanket. You've also been aware of buoys sporting seaweed skirts, (matching the one on your dinghy); and that your waterline is likewise fringed with growth.

Even more indicative that the days for boating are dwindling down to a precious few, you have been conscious of loneliness; of missing the cheerful company of other boats. A fleet previously winnowed only slightly, is now considerably thinned. Indeed, so prevalent are winter moorings, (some of them hardly discernible at high tide), you find you have to be more than usually careful when navigating your harbor. How shorn boats look without their masts; how mournful, somehow, to see other spars being pulled at a dock. Even the 210s and the Thunderbirds have vanished and with them their spinnakers, as bright in their billowing (during the last few informal races) as bubbles of colored glass.

Should you essay a final cruise, you find the same empty waters (with the exception of a party boat or two and the lobstermen and the ferries, only an occasional other small craft like your own remains), the same bare beaches and boarded cottages, the same ghost towns in what just lately were busy ports. If these signs aren't enough to tell you that it's time to be hauled, shorter days proclaim it. As do skies teeming with migrating fowl.

As always, the last run of the year to your yacht yard is bleak, rough, and bitterly cold. Bundled up like Polar explorers, you wallow for its duration in gray swells—to starboard a landscape etched in amethyst, behind you a horizon black as doom. And ahead? There, in the Indian summer that (perversely) will now appear, lie the unloading of your boat, the storing of its gear (did you really have all that equipment aboard?), the winterizing of the engine, the covering of the hull. Sad tasks all. And yet deeper than any feeling of sadness will be that of satisfaction over a season accomplished. One good in and for itself.

And prelude—if possible—to an even better *next*.

On a Sojourn South

THOUSANDS HAVE TRANSITED THE INTRACOASTAL Waterway but the first time *you* do it is the first time it's ever been done. Departing the marina at James Landing in Scituate in late September aboard *Sea Story II,* Warren and I didn't know whether or not we'd make our intended destination of Jacksonville, Florida.

Seven days earlier Hurricane Hugo had slammed into Charleston, South Carolina, and environs, wreaking incalculable damage and raising tremendous doubts as to the itinerary of the trip we'd planned for so long. Before quitting Scituate, Warren had called the Charleston Coast Guard several times, but no hard facts as to conditions in the confusing aftermath of the storm were really ascertainable. So much energy, time, and thought—not to mention money—had been invested in the venture, we decided to play the trip by ear and to get as far south as we could. In a way this uncertainty as to outcome added to the excitement of the proceedings.

For adventure it proved to be—and idyll—and ordeal, not necessarily in the ways we'd envisioned.

Let me state at the outset that we did make Jacksonville, arriving on Saturday, October 21, having accomplished a journey of 1,265 miles. En route we recorded 147 engine hours, during which we burned 1,162 gallons of fuel at eight gallons an hour and making an average speed of nine knots. Roughly, the twenty-four-day voyage broke down into two segments, with entirely different challenges and impressions: the first two weeks from Scituate to Norfolk, Virginia; and the last eleven days on the ICW from Portsmouth, Virginia, to Jacksonville. The worst part of the journey was getting ready for it: a monumental undertaking encompassing every sort of provision and store for a month. Friends who had made this trip many times suggested that unless we wanted to live on hot dogs and bologna sandwiches we bring as much of our own food as possible. In a freezer my husband designed and had installed under a corner seat in our cabin, we froze meats enough for three weeks, and only had to replenish milk, bread, and produce along the way.

In the spring we had moved up from a Grand Banks thirty-two to the thirty-six, equipping her with twin Cummins 210 diesel engines and a full range of electronics including a two-station loran-C; radar with guard zone alarm; two VHF radios; depth sounder with remote; and an autopilot with a flybridge override. And all summer we had spent in shakedown cruises in our local waters.

The first half of our journey was a wear-and-tear odyssey interspersed with images of utter glory. It was almost continuously cold, windy, and rough. Twenty miles out of Scituate the breeze picked up and thereafter hardly ever stopped blowing. So rude were its blasts in the Cape Cod Canal we took down the bimini and never raised it again until well into the South. So turbulent was Buzzard's Bay on our second day that we returned to the port of Padanaram; sorrowed to learn later that a sailor had been swept off a sloop and lost southeast of Block Island that day in winds of thirty-five knots and seas of eight to ten feet. On subsequent legs Rhode Island and Long Island Sounds were also sloppy, as were New York Harbor and the New Jersey coast. A twenty-five-knot hard northwesterly and breaking three- to four-foot seas forced us into Atlantic Highlands, New Jersey, in midmorning after our departure one day from Weehawken; and on the next the Sandy Hook Channel was even wilder. Three times— from Atlantic City to Cape May, up the forty-eight miles of Delaware Bay, and down the final hundred miles of the Chesapeake to Norfolk —the skipper had to run the boat from inside and below—as it was just too wet topside. With our windows underwater much of the time and our flybridge showered with flying spray, our staunch yacht seemed like nothing so much as a bucking bronco in a carwash of salt!

The dress of the day every day for most of the first two weeks was heavy jackets, woolen hats, mittens, double socks (and pantyhose for the first mate). Consistently icy mornings followed frigid nights, and we would rise to find a boat completely beaded with condensation, which slick required at least ten minutes and many paper towels to absorb. Wind always adds to the workload, and particularly bitter blasts. Our feet were always blocks of ice, as were our fingers whenever exposed. Mine got used to being burned upon departure from coiling lines that were the next thing to dry ice. Adding to the chill were twilights of a hard pink, and the fact that it was dark practically at dinnertime. (Ironically, the sharpest cold of the cruise we endured on a day of record cold in Georgia—during a ninety-three-mile passage from Thunderbolt to St. Simon's Island—most of it out in the middle of nowhere—and all of it with subfreezing temperatures, winds of thirty knots, sea smoke, and a terrible chop.)

Besides the layday in Padanaram, weather or engine problems forced delays in three other ports. A slight leak in our fuel injector pump was attended to in Norwalk, Connecticut; a "fried" port alternator—removed and diagnosed as failed at Solomons, Maryland—had to be replaced by a Cummins dealer in Portsmouth, Virginia (after a nasty nine-hour slug to get there on one alternator). A starboard door warped just enough to let in water, a shorted windshield wiper, and another which grated like an Indian's war whoop would wait until winter for their repairs.

One stunning positive can make up for a host

of negatives, and affirmatives we had aplenty. Leaving by dawn each day, we were granted one sumptuous sunrise after another. As *Sea Story II* plied her way by the Sakonnet, and thence Newport, Point Judith, and Westerly and into Fishers Island Sound we became reacquainted with the joys of "coasting." Lighthouses were another delight along with racing sailboats. A fleet of J/24s burgeoned out of nowhere off Stratford, Connecticut; with other flotillas bending this way and that outside of Annapolis. To say nothing of the happening that is New York Harbor. Never the same port twice, there is a glamour here you find nowhere else on the water. Autumn's special splendor must be included in these pluses; as should solid, state-of-the-art docks (such as those at Farley's Marina at Atlantic City); the sportive ambience of ports like Cape May; and the blessings of shelter and calm on certain legs and in several canals.

The Intracoastal Waterway, we discovered, as we wended our way through the states of Virginia, North and South Carolina, Georgia and Florida, is a maze of rivers, creeks, canals, cuts, sounds, inlets, and bays. So narrow, shallow, and winding is much of it you rarely can use your autopilot; and indeed, concentration has to be continuous so as not to go aground or astray. Here, the ICW widens out to an expanse seemingly broad as the ocean (on Albemarle Sound in North Carolina, for example); there, it tapers to a strait so tight it isn't safe to pass another vessel. Portions of it remind you of an expressway because of their flatness and breadth. Now you navigate a desolate stretch—or else a built-up run—or you bang for hours across a sound. Many a passage features currents: head currents, reversing currents, currents from inlets, currents flowing through marinas or under bridges, some so furious it's like fording rapids to make your way against them.

The water itself, we noticed in Norfolk Harbor (somewhat startled at the brown froth of our wake), is tea-colored from all the tannic acid of the area's vegetation; and within a week *Sea Story II* had sprouted yellow whiskers. A good deal of the country is swampy southern Gothic—a wilderness of amber ditches lined with eerie trees and studded with stumps and sticks. (Of man-made debris we happily saw little, with what refuse there was almost entirely natural.) Piloting the Alligator River and the Alligator River/Pungo River Canal we felt like Bogie and Hepburn aboard the *African Queen,* so wild and tangled was the topography. Also evoking this tropical note were trees with shapes exotic as the plane trees in Africa and fanning into great canopies along North Carolina's Bogue Sound; plus palms and stands of pampas grass and the kudzu that draped itself like a dark and spongy dropcloth along many a banking.

If sandbars to all sides (and often close aboard) were common, and mile after pastoral mile of marsh—so were bridges. Earlier, we had been impressed with the mammoths of the East River and Verrazano Narrows, and particularly with the awesome span over the Chesapeake, but what the bridges of the South lacked in grandeur, they more than made up for in numbers. The ICW seemed one continuum of bridges—swing bridges; bascules; lift bridges and fixed. Bridges that were drawn or moved on pontoons; that opened on demand or only according to set schedules. Bridges at which you drifted and waited and were surprised sometimes to meet old friends. Confusing bridges where several channels and shallow waters and rushing currents and not much time to decide exactly how to proceed converged. Bridges on which you nicked your antenna or held it down to avoid a repetition.

Don't attempt the Intracoastal if you're cowed by tugs. Large and small, they crowd the waterways, often appearing with almost no notice because of the twisting terrain. Out on the open ocean and in the ample sounds and harbors of the upper East Coast there is plenty of room to maneuver, but from Portsmouth down, there simply isn't the space. With little warning here comes a workhorse—pushing or hauling a barge or loaded with sand and gravel or trucks or containers—or "deadheading" back to its base. All of the tugboat skippers sound (you'd swear) like Johnny Cash and conduct their communications on channel 13 without preliminaries. They know the waterway like the back of their hand and their counsel should be heeded—as we did *Island Boy*'s in South Carolina's Pine Island Cut, waiting for his okay (and a curve he knew was coming) before we ventured to pass.

Along the ICW you learn to make way while you can, because you can't very often. Not only do NO WAKE signs abound, so do anglers in boats and on bankings, and mile after mile of dwellings with decks with docked and tethered small craft. If the incredible shallowness south of Norfolk had surprised us, so did our continually having to power down so as not to swamp or capsize the multitude of locals who were fishing literally everywhere and most in modest boats with almost no freeboard. Though people fish in the north, they fish in numbers nowhere near the scores that they do in the South. In Morehead City, North Carolina, in mid-October at least you would think you were in Dunkirk, so extensive was the flotilla. Motoring down the ICW is nothing if not an exercise in discipline and patience, for this plethora of fisherfolk seems placed fiendishly to thwart your forward progress. One of the most constant images you encounter is that of yellow bobbers floating on the surface with hard by a couple in a small tin boat hauling in a net. In Myrtle Grove Sound, we were dumbstruck by the sight of a tug that actually had to stop in midchannel for one of these innumerable small craft, in no hurry whatever to pull in his catch and get out of the way.

Earlier, in the Chesapeake and Delaware Canal, we had become aware of the considerable wake our Grand Banks created (even when going a reasonable speed) when a man on shore standing by his small boat "docked" up out of the water and ostensibly out of the wash had waved wildly to us to "slow down!" Which admonition had been repeated in Portsmouth's Elizabeth River when a police boat had told us to cut our eight-knot speed to six.

Official and otherwise, a network of "watchers" abets this control. Self-appointed vigilantes get on channel 13 and warn boats heading south too fast (by their standards anyway) that they are going to be hauled into court, which notification is couched in very colorful language indeed, most of it blue. Some minutes after *Sea Story II*'s passing of a small marina on the Waccamaw River in South Carolina we heard the manager radioing the Georgetown Coast Guard to intercept a large sportfisherman behind us because he had roared full bore by their piers, heedless of everything and everybody including exceptionally high water due to an abnormally high tide, and had ignored their radio call to boot. The next thing we knew the Georgetown Coast Guard was coming upriver, checking the name on each boat as it passed, looking for the offender (who also hadn't responded when hailed and railed at by another boat for passing *him* improperly; as the sportfisherman had managed to do with *Sea Story II* the day before, gunning his boat unbelievably in a narrow gut bounded by cottages and all kinds of craft). Evidently the renegade was caught and cited, for he never tore by again.

Some fellow travelers because of greater boat speed, eventually pulled away; others, slower than you, inevitably fell behind. "Peer" boats were encountered time and again. Now yachts might be gathered at bridges or docks; now you were alone; but always you sensed the procession heading south. Sometimes a vessel in a slot too pinched to pass would be going too slowly, holding up a whole procession to his stern. Or an unthinking skipper would pin you down on a pier for general conversation when you were busy trying to tie your ship up to its poles or scrub it down. Other mariners were help itself with dock lines in crowded situations complicated by currents; or in permitting you to raft (as we had to do at the Atlantic Yacht Basin in Virginia); or in guiding you through a maze of marks in a heavily trafficked sound.

We were grateful, too, for the blessings of warmth after cold and smooth waters after rude. How welcome were temperatures in the seven-

ties and eighties with bright sun and blue skies
and calm channels and crossings of sounds. (Even
the Albemarle, reputedly rough, raised hardly a
ripple.) Fees for dockage were another delight
(much lower than in the North), as was our first
trip in a golf cart to a supermarket. Traveling at a
speed of about four mph with the first mate act-
ing as the rearview mirror, off we went to downtown Belhaven, North Carolina, our carrier com-
pliments of our marina.

They say you can't go south without going
aground—and we did, briefly, twice. En route to
Beaufort, from Charleston—and running the boat
in heavy rain and from below—while squaring
away some charts and on a long stretch between
marks, we drifted too far to port on a river and
bounced *Sea Story II* into a mud bank (the first
time either of our Grand Banks had ever touched
bottom!). By Warren's instinctively going to neutral and idle, her bow dropped and she surfed over
the bar and came right into deeper water—her
props and shafts protected by her massive hull and
skeg. With heart in mouth the skipper slowly
accelerated both shafts up to 2,200 rpms and happily felt no more than the usual thrums and trem-
bles of that speed. The second grounding also

occurred in foul weather while shifting to the lower station near a range somewhere in Georgia; with *Sea Story II* this time backing off into the channel, forgiving her crew their momentary lapse, her loyal engines never missing a beat.

Like the North, the South served up a stream of memorable impressions. Fascinating, bustling Norfolk was a wonder with its bevies of ships of every sort, and its booms, barges, and cranes in constant motion. The lock at Great Bridge, Virginia, was managed with a minimum of fuss, thanks to the competence and courtesy of the men who manned that chamber. There were the eerie aesthetics of an early-morning transit of the Albemarle and Chesapeake Canal through mists so luminous they were almost unearthly; and the chimera presented by the largest tug with the longest tow we'd ever glimpsed—an image of incandescent majesty as, brilliantly lit, it motored up the Waccamaw River long after midnight. Not forgetting Beaufort, South Carolina's, gracious "Gone With the Wind" wealth of mansions and massive oaks swathed in Spanish moss; or strings of pelicans or sporting dolphins.

Words always bow their heads before the deepest feelings so this crew barely spoke as we viewed

Charleston. On October 5 at Atlantic City we had heard the first and only VHF radio report about the condition of the ICW in South Carolina, namely that it was open but full of debris. Even when we left Bucksport on the 17th—bound for Charleston—we didn't know what we would find. (We had discussed options with the marina manager at Bucksport, deciding to take his advice and go to Charleston with the intention of anchoring somewhere in the environs.) En route in Four Mile Creek Canal we had passed one limping fish boat towing another. We next went by mile after mile of rusted pines, wondering if their red color could be salt burn from the hurricane? Then came a bleak and battered stretch by McClellanville leading to the absolute devastation at the little settlement at the Francis Marion National Forest Recreation Area on Harbor River—smashed and leveled so completely the country looked like a no-man's-land. Acre upon razed acre followed of trees torn up and toppled and tumbled like twigs; of houses totally flattened or partially destroyed; of boats wracked up and ruined on shores and in woods and fields. The havoc had to be seen to be believed. As we powered slowly by the Isle of Palms and a pier piled high with ravaged yachts, so tender and sore still was that locale that someone ashore asked us to shift into neutral and "glide through on idle."

After making our way across a windy and busy Charleston Harbor we tied up at the last "slip" in the port's only open marina (the Ripley Light)—port side to a grounded rusty barge sans power or water and with a damaged fifty-four-foot motor-yacht on a cradle atop it—a unique berth in twenty years of cruising, and grateful we were to get it! All the rest of that day and until well after dark boats kept pouring into the marina to be fueled and then rafted, with seven thousand gallons pumped on that one day alone.

If some of our sojourn had been neither comfortable nor pleasant—all of it had been instructive; and taken as a whole it had been a transfiguring episode—for every goal achieved is a gateway to another. From the sublime to the infinitely sobering we had run the gamut of experience, with every instant from the Verrazano Narrows Bridge south an unknown. Good teamwork and a fine trawler had contributed to our success, and flying north to Massachusetts we looked forward, we "snowbirds," to returning to Florida come spring and to bringing *Sea Story II* back home.

On the Deeps of Winter

THE BLUES ARE DEEPER; THE WHITES SHARPER; the golds icicle-cold in the winters on the coast. Lighthouses that look dreamy in summer have now an arctic cast—and the absolute clarity that is the gift of subfreezing temperatures. Stacked on docks are lobster pots along with troves of brightly painted buoys. Gray waves break upon bleak shores beneath a blustery scud. But the sea is silver, too, and ledge jet-black as day declines. The elemental forms stand firm—as great trees rear above the granite rocks in which they've sunken roots. In substance and symbol the coast endures—and sustains and inspires.

Vessels have long since been winterized; covered (or not) as the skipper determined; stored indoors, in the yards of marinas (or at home), or left in the water. Yachts that spend the winter outside are soon mantled with snow or frozen fast in ice. Like neighbors they seem to commune as they quietly wait. A few are decked with the season's greenings; while some look ghostly —white hulls against white ground and skies. So swaddled are other craft as they rest on cradles they resemble mummies.

Fish boats, a bevy of which continue to drag and haul, stand out bright red or orange on the stark blue seas. You notice now the beauty of their snow-flocked rigging and seines. Indeed, the forms of piers and poles, of pulpits and masts appear to be etched, so strictly are their lines defined.

Mariners fill this interim visiting showrooms or studying catalogs or reading the nautical novels they've saved; dreaming, as they do, of the delights of the spring that's almost, they insist, on doorstep and dock.

On Creative Accommodation

SOME OF US ARE NOT SAILORS SO MUCH AS THE mates of mariners. For our spouses, the ocean is both a glory and a need; for us, a taste acquired so that we might keep our helpmates company.

It used to be that I felt guilty about my lack of interest in the bread-and-butter aspects of boating: in the charting, the navigating, the operation and routine maintenance of our boat. Such limitations trouble me no longer. Apart from the charting (and I can read a chart, I hasten to add), I hold up my own end in those other "nuts-and-bolts" departments, even though many a task is not inherently absorbing. And I contribute in

other ways. I'm the somebody there who can take
up the slack. That extra pair of eyes, ears, and
hands. Afloat, I serve as my husband's sounding
board as he does for me when ashore. Sometimes
I help through being patient; at others, through
being ready to take a reasonable risk; or through
not panicking even if I don't intuit immediately
how to best aid in this situation or that.

But there are other more positive pleasures for
one who is not a sailor through and through. I
love the travel part of boating, and especially the
exploration of our ports of call. If my husband's
passion is for the sea, mine is for country. For the
poetry of lawns and gardens, of shady sidewalks
and streets. For all their Puritan spirit, the harbors of New England exhibit a charm almost
wanton, and I, for one, never tire of touring
them. Intensely involved with others ordinarily, I
find that to walk about unrecognized in unfamiliar places is a sort of wandering of green pastures.
Those leisurely rambles in which I can study
houses, yards, shops, people—whatever com-
prises the life native to the place but fresh and
new to myself—are to me the heart of the cruising experience.

Often, I also welcome what is "daring" about

the activity. There are certain voyages so exciting you can't regret them, even if you have to spend the balance of the day sleeping off the tension of the passage. That minute when the skipper turns into a stiff wind so that you can take down sails, kneeling on the bow and hanging for dear life onto the pulpit as the deck goes up and down beneath you; the steep slope of your vessel in a decided heel; reaching farther than you ever have before into territory that is virginal and lonely (east of Petit Manan, for instance); proceeding cautiously through fog, every cell in your body alert for any sight or sound; essaying channels like Woods Hole that demand total concentration and leave little room for mistakes—call out the adventurer in your soul.

Beauty is another crystal spring infusing the sport with delight. Its manifestations are everywhere. In a rising cherry-colored sun. In the red wink of an aid after dark. In ducks in ragged wedges. In pastel dwellings climbing a hill. In windjammers white as snow against the bluegreen loom of Mount Desert. In the figures of clammers, simple as those painted by Millet or van Gogh. In sandbars like brown-edged cookies. In the dark blue waters of spring. In summer's shimmering seas and autumn's fiery shores. In clouds of sparkling sea smoke in the winter.

Some intensely negative feelings I found myself struggling with off and on in my relation to the sea have long since been resolved. Apprehension as to conditions has been largely allayed by sheer experience. Though you've never seen it all, after a certain number of years of cruising, you've seen a good variety of weather. Familiarity does dull somewhat the terror of malevolent elements. By choice, however, by as careful a monitoring as possible of forecasts, and by the exercise of common sense, we endure few wretched passages.

Concern as to consequences has been eased by the purchase of safety gear and through the practice of certain procedures. For both comfort's and safety's sake, we indulge in "redundancy." In the days when we were sailing, in addition to our engine we had four sails (including a main with two sets of reef points, giving us three sails in one; and a two-sails-in-one reefing genoa). We had a weather radio and a weather band on our RDF. We had a steering compass and a good hand-bearing compass. We had life jackets, life vests (which we wore in the fog), flotation jackets, harnesses (which we donned as a matter of course in winds of twenty or more knots). We had a dinghy with which we could abandon ship. Besides batteries to start our engine, we had a backup hand crank. And two anchors: one with three-quarter-inch line, another with half-inch line. If our depth sounder broke down, we had a marked anchor line that we could use for a lead line. We had a VHF radio and a flare kit; two airhorns. Should the skipper be incapacitated or otherwise engaged, I could operate the radio; I knew how to anchor; how to close seacocks. Our plan of action for overboard persons was regularly practiced. Now that we are cruising in a Grand Banks trawler yacht we are no less "redundant," with two lorans, two radios, two compasses among our aids and equipment.

Though you can't legislate love for a sport any more than for a person, in my case affection for my husband led me to consciously "accentuate the positive" in my attitude toward the boating he relishes. Desertion was never an option. The sea is at the center of my husband's nature. To leave him alone on it would be to share only surfaces, not the substance of ourselves. Such an abdication can spell death to a relationship. I knew I didn't want to settle for endurance. Bearing your lot may be better than not bearing it, but it's still a poor substitute for enjoyment. Since I have a healthy amount of pride and self-respect, neither did I want to be one of those women who is a care and nuisance to others and a disappointment to herself.

Toward this end, I set up certain goals as a sort of text for my conduct. Though I make my feelings known, because I am always a little reluctant to leave a port when the weather isn't fair, I try never to manipulate out of fear (and if we're honest with ourselves we *know* when we're knuckling under to a timidity to which we ought not give scope). I also try not to succumb to sloth, that psychic paralysis that can grip you if you let it; but instead to train myself to be a more active participant, one who "turns to" automatically, without being prompted or reminded.

Creative accommodation is easy when the one inspiring it is an almost ideal skipper. If my husband has a cast-iron stomach and steady nerves, a seemingly inexhaustible strength (along with an absolute practical grasp), he also has *heart*—a depth of human understanding that makes all the difference. Not only is he endlessly thoughtful—maneuvering the boat so that I can take pictures, getting me a paper, putting up the canopy (when we were sailing) as soon as possible for his sun-sensitive wife—he is also tolerant of my limitations. (My hesitancy about jumping on docks I feel are too high or too low for a thoughtless leap; my sometimes awkward flailing when picking up moorings; my anxieties about getting this bow line around that piling or whether he will jump back aboard in time from the dock and not leave me alone at the helm.)

If dread has for the most part been banished, discomforts are also kept to a minimum. As you do with the elements, you learn to "play" your own nature. Since my eyes go eight different directions at once when too long below while underway, I keep such visits brief. The heat, which more than anything else can level me, is countered by a number of measures—the proper clothing and protective ointments; the avoidance of undue exposure; the swims (in the middle of a passage we sometimes drift and take a dunk); the darkened cabin; the bimini (these days instead of a canopy); the cold drinks; the remaining aboard when it is cooler on your mooring than anywhere else in the harbor and heat exhaustion is a real possibility. If the anchorage is too dirty for swimming, I "dive" below and put on shorts, peeling off boat shoes and kerchief-and-hat (the former used to secure the latter headgear and both that much more protection from the sun).

Ignorance, however, is the biggest discomfort. There is no woe quite like that of feeling yourself helpless. Blatant ignorance is also arrogant—like living in a foreign country and remaining oblivious of its language and customs. A lack of technical skills and innate wind sense can be improved deliberately, and simply through the doing, I learned when we were sailing. Just as a stone is worn smooth by the water, some of your roughest edges disappear from continued immersion in the activity. I no longer had to think so much about what I did (like which way to push the tiller when my husband told me to "fall off" or "head up"). We're forever discussing "rules of the road" as different circumstances present themselves. "I'm supposed to fall off and go astern of him, right?" I'd check with the skipper when I was at the helm in a crossing situation. Or—well in advance of a change of direction (in both our sail- and powerboats)—"I know. Turn early and turn *big!*"—signaling clearly thereby to another vessel where I intend to go. Though you don't have to be a "waterphile" or an expert sailor to enjoy the water, you're more apt to enjoy it, I've discovered, as your skills improve.

The passivity I used at times to find insufferable, I'm now almost grateful for. In the press of modern life there are very few hours left for reverie and reflection. Those dull, necessary passages when you are just far enough offshore not to see very much can be a time of sorting things out. People who cruise a lot together are often silent in a companionable way. There's so much talk in most of our lives that it's a relief now and then not to have to listen or speak.

Purchasing a 35mm camera also aided in the dispelling of ennui, for it helped me, both literally and figuratively, to focus on the beauty, drama, challenge, and complex interests of cruising. One happy offshoot of this "recording" of the life in harbors and underway was the eventual founding of my own stock photo agency, with many marine periodicals as regular clients for my work.

The benefits netted from the decision to commit myself to the constructive are almost too numerous to chronicle. Boating has helped me plumb my own character with all its pros and cons. It has taught me that I'm not made out of tissue paper. Though we never seek the adverse, I have been rather proud, on occasion, of having endured the tempestuous. It has taken a nature too much at home in observing life and forced it to act. It has helped me to nurture another's gladness of soul. How often the set of my husband's body at tiller or wheel has spoken of his joy in contention. It has helped us meld successfully as couple and crew.

The many agreeable people that you meet I count as another plus. Also the handful of "characters," and all those who comprise what might be called the "human comedy" side of cruising (exemplified by anchoring and mooring foibles in which no person is injured or property damaged). Boating has caused me to marvel, as well, at the exploits of those explorers of yore. Men who ventured strange seas and shores without the aid of accurate charts, modern instruments and materials, and weather forecasts. Men who relied on—and triumphed through—the truly essential attributes of the human senses, mind, and spirit.

Boating gives you something to talk about. (Mention any aspect of the sport to a real sailor and you have his absolute attention.) It makes geography come alive. We have cruised it so often the whole coast of New England is like a road map in my mind. It enables you to experience perfection. Sailing at its best—in a wind of twelve to fourteen knots, say, and on a sapphire sea strewn with brilliants—is one of the purest of the physical sensations: an ultimate.

Just as you are put more in touch with your own emotions on the ocean, so your experience of the weather is more direct; your knowledge of the seasons more complete; your acquaintance with wildlife that much more intimate.

The boating that helps to satisfy my love of the outdoors is one of its most varied sports, combining the pleasures of land and sea. A mariner can step off his yacht and onto a bus. He can hire a cab or a car. He can golf, fish, hike, jog, play tennis— and then return to his vessel and sail or steam away. And travel on the water is frequently more beautiful than highway transit. Sojourning by automobile, how many times are you apt to cry: "What a pretty car!"? By contrast, how often during a voyage we are wonderstruck by the loveliness of a passing windship or a handsome motoryacht.

Other boons? The air is better on the water. And in the heat of the summer you are usually where the breeze is.

That my husband's interest in boating is organic and immediate and mine aesthetic and evolving does not invalidate either. Indeed, taken as a whole they constitute one continuum of enjoyment. Lucky the crewmates whose differences don't divide—but enlarge, instead—and unite.

On Taking Stock

AFTER THE HUMAN SHARING WITH THE SKIPPER, I am grateful for the skills of all those people none of us could boat without (since no mariner can be completely self-sufficient). For yacht-yard personnel who haul, launch, and repair our vessels. For the mooring services who maintain our gear. For the harbormasters who "run a tight port," and the launch drivers who ferry us about. For marina staffs who offer slips and water, fuel, oil, and ice (and sometimes fish and lobsters!). For the bridgekeepers who raise their spans to grant us clearance. And for the Coast Guard, always at the ready to rescue or help.

Race committees, too—who set the marks, start the races, and log the finishers—deserve recognition; as do the crewmates willing to be hoisted aloft or to dive, if need be, beneath the boat.

I rejoice in the ever-expanding role of women on the water. No longer relegated to simply tending to the young and to cooking, provisioning, and such, some now crew on fish boats, sail single-handedly around the world, own and operate their own yachts—or, as licensed captains, pilot ships.

Boating discourse by itself can enlighten and amuse. There is many a wry quip or pithy comment to be heard on the VHF radio. "We've had so much rain we've got mushrooms growing up from the keel," laments one mariner. "Pretty day, pretty bay," muses another. "Get off 16!" yells an "enforcer" who, one suspects, probably never leaves the dock.

I am thankful for the innumerable pleasures investing cruising. For vistas stretched like murals before our eyes. For a solid mooring, a sheltered passage, a spanking southeast breeze. For laydays with their dressing up and dining out and strolls through the green evenings of summer.

For all the things we learn I also give thanks. (Aware that the greater the knowledge, the more informed the decisions.) Gazing at a "ranging" horizon you know it's going to be rough. Any cruise will be a mix, you long ago discovered, but good or bad the condition is transient. This port is to be avoided because of its surge; that one entered early so as not to be "skunked." The least-private anchorage? The most secluded, since the fewer the boats, the closer the scrutiny. (Whereas in busy harbors you're lost in the crowd.)

Our reliance on charts and the aids-to-navigation that serve as signposts on the sea can't be overstated. Indebted we are to nun buoys and cans; to bell, gong, and whistle buoys; to junction and midchannel buoys; to day beacons, minor lights, and automated lighthouses—all of which promote our safety afloat.

Most profoundly, perhaps, I value the fundamentals—the moon and stars in their places; the patterns of the tides; the topography and geography (apart from shifting sandbars and channels and erosion) that remain, in the main, the same. When Henry Hudson's *Half Moon* entered the Hudson River there was no George Washington Bridge or twin Trade Towers, but there *was* a Manhattan Island and the Palisades on the New Jersey shore. When the *Mayflower* dropped its hook in Provincetown (prior to crossing Cape Cod Bay to Plymouth), there was no breakwater nor monument, but Long Point was there along with a sculpted landscape of scrub pine and dunes.

How bountiful is boating! Just when you think it can't present you with another good, it does—and that time and again. For these and countless other blessings—those that have been and those that are to be—I salute and celebrate our sport—and the sea.